When solicitation for the $70 million Queen's Challenge Campaign was completed in the summer of 1993, the tally surpassed $100 million. Such an achievement can only be attained through exemplary teamwork. Thanks to your efforts as a key volunteer, Queen's is well positioned for this competitive decade. Congratulations and thank you for your support of Queen's University.

- Allan R. Taylor, Campaign Chairman

Queen's

hedgehog productions

The First One Hundred & Fifty Years

Copyright ©1990 Hedgehog Productions Inc.

Canadian Cataloguing in Publication Data

Carpenter, Thomas, 1959—
   Queen's: the first one hundred & fifty years

ISBN 1-895261-01-5 (leather bound)
ISBN 1-895261-00-7

1. Queen's University (Kingston, Ont.)—History.
I. Title.

LE3.Q32C37   1990   378.713'72   C90-095009-9

Trade distribution by Firefly Books, 250 Sparks Avenue, Willowdale, Ontario, Canada M2H 2S4

Printed in Canada for Hedgehog Productions Inc., P.O. Box 129, Newburgh, Ontario K0K 2S0

Design by
Q Kumquat Designs

Colour separations by
Hadwen Graphics
Ottawa, Ontario

Printed and bound in Canada by
D.W. Friesen & Sons
Altona, Manitoba

Printed on acid-free paper

Publisher: Frank B. Edwards

Editor: Thomas H. Carpenter

Art Director: Linda J. Menyes

Photography: Alan Carruthers, J.A. Kraulis, Ernie Sparks, Jack Chiang

Editorial Advisor: F.W. Gibson

Production: Laurel Aziz, Catherine DeLury, Peggy Denard, Patricia Denard-Hinch, Susan Dickinson, Laura Elston, Christine Kulyk, Janice McLean, Mary Patton, Tracy C. Read and Debi Wells

Alumni Resource Committee: Jim Bennett, Ken Cuthbertson, Herb Hamilton, Alison Holt, Mary Lou Marlin, Cathy Perkins and Pat Smith

Acknowledgements

All who worked on *Queen's: The First One Hundred & Fifty Years* wish to express their sincere gratitude to the dozens of people within the Queen's community who, for over a year and a half, answered our questions, gave directions, unearthed obscure pieces of information, occasionally bent the rules and generally provided assistance to the researchers, writers and photographers working on this project.

We wish to give well-deserved credit to Dr. Jim Bennett and Pat Smith of the Department of Alumni Affairs and to the staff of the *Queen's Alumni Review*, Ken Cuthbertson, Alison Holt and Mary Lou Marlin, and former editors Cathy Perkins and the late Dr. Herb Hamilton. They not only conceived the idea of a book to celebrate the University's 150th anniversary but also participated in the design, editing and production of this work.

Further, we wish to thank Frederick W. Gibson, Emeritus Professor of History and the author of *Queen's University, Volume II, 1917-1961, To Serve and Yet Be Free*, for his ongoing assistance and for his patience and encouragement. And while the editors, of course, bear sole responsibility for any mistakes that remain, we also wish to thank Professor Gibson for so often steering us clear of error.

And, finally, we want to emphasize the essential role played in this project by the Queen's University Archives and to offer our sincere thanks. Without these facilities and the assistance of staff members Anne MacDermaid, George Henderson, Dr. Shirley Spragge, Paul Banfield, Margaret Bignell, Stewart Renfrew, Bruce Riggs, Heather Wolsey and Susan Office, this book could not have been produced.

Well-worn Queen's crest

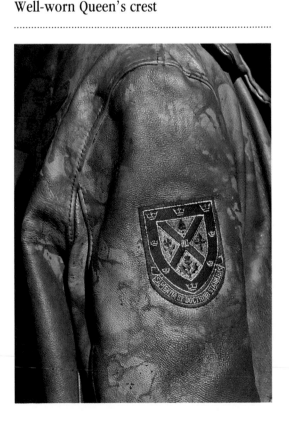

Chancellor's Introduction

One of the rewards of an official celebration such as Queen's Sesquicentennial is the opportunity it provides to recognize past achievements and to address future challenges. The University's first 150 years have coincided with great social and technical changes, and the next century and a half will be no less revolutionary.

Conceived at a time when continental railroads, telephones, electric lights and air travel seemed the stuff of fantasy, Queen's grew to maturity alongside the nation it has served so well. As the world changed, so did the institution. To the already well-established degrees in Arts, Theology, Medicine and Science were added such contemporary disciplines as engineering, education, commerce, law, nursing, urban and regional planning, physical education and fine arts. As advances in communications technology brought the concept of the global village ever closer to reality, Queen's responded to society's new expectations. The computers that are propelling the world in a thousand new directions continue to transform the nature of teaching and research at Queen's and, in turn, are themselves changed by our scholars.

One of the most profound revolutions of this century is the changing status of women, and as I write these words, a new kind of national emancipation is giving women a stronger voice on our campus. In today's world, our University in Kingston is widely sought by international students from many continents, as well as by students from every corner of Canada. Queen's Scottish Presbyterian roots and 150-year-old trunk are branching out — as its founders envisioned — to provide equal access to the privilege of learning to people of all nationalities and cultures. The changing faces and races of our students enrich each other's lives. Together, they share the excellent teaching and research opportunities that Queen's affords.

Queen's Chancellors, of whom there have been nine before me, have been men of great vision and other fine qualities. As for myself, I am a person of the present. I am not a clairvoyant. However, in contemplating the next 150 years, I can truly say that as a Queen's woman born and a Queen's woman bred, I have every confidence that when our 300th anniversary is celebrated, Queen's will still be a winner. *Cha Gheill!*
— Agnes McCausland Benidickson

Chancellor Agnes McCausland Benidickson

6

Chancellor Emeritus's Introduction

I became a fan of Queen's University on October 27, 1923, the day that Queen's defeated McGill's football team. A graduate of the University of Alberta, I had just returned to Canada as a barrister after three years at Hertford College, Oxford.

The bleachers were full that day, and Queen's boasted such champions as Batstone, Evans, Leadlay and McKelvey. Football woke me up and won me over to Queen's, a school with a string of continuing victories that proved discomfiting to McGill, Toronto and the University of Western Ontario.

Football, however, has not been my only tie to the University. In the course of my duties as Speaker of the House of Commons, I was invited in 1958, with the Speaker of the Senate, to receive a Doctorate of Laws. That made me a true member of the Queen's community with status and rights as an alumnus that I value highly.

Later, during my time as Governor General of Canada, two leading Principals (John Deutsch and Ronald Watts) assured me that I would be welcomed as Chancellor when I became free for the post. In April 1974, at a special convocation, I was installed as Chancellor; for the next six years, I presided over convocations and the annual meetings of the Queen's University Council.

It is clear that the development of Queen's has owed much to the Principals, Trustees, professors and graduates who, by their determination that it should survive and make a distinctive contribution to Canada, laid the foundation for the Queen's of today. Their realization that the University was a vital link in Canada's development inspired many graduates to lead Canada into nationhood — and the 20th century.

And now, as the 21st century approaches, Queen's celebrates its 150th anniversary — a significant milestone for a school built on the edge of the frontier. In many ways, its evolution has parallelled that of Canada, growing from modest roots into an important institution despite the inevitable conflicts and rivalries that surround the development of any such enterprise.

Yet thankfully, for all its advances and accomplishments, Queen's University has not strayed far from its founders' original dream. Still at Kingston, it is beloved by those who pass through its doors and respected across Canada and around the world.
— The Right Honourable Roland Michener

The Right Honourable Roland Michener

Preface

In 150 years of activity, more than 70,000 students have passed through Queen's University and come under the influence of thousands of professors and administrators. The people of Queen's have spent their prodigious energies in the pursuit of higher learning, in the pursuit of truths and progress and sometimes, it must be admitted, in the pursuit of the merest follies. They have investigated everything under the sun and, in discussion, have ranged even further afield than that. They have studied, made merry, fought food fights and embraced the eternal verities. Generation upon generation of students, living out some of the most important years of their lives, have passed into adulthood while attending Queen's, and although people come and go, a university retains some small part of everyone who studies there, and memories of the individuals fill up the traditions of the institution. From that deep well of history and anecdote, the editors of *Queen's: The First One Hundred & Fifty Years* have chosen their stories, and here, they offer a mosaic — stories arranged into the patterns of life and tradition during one and a half centuries at Queen's University.

As is inevitable in a book of this kind, far more has been left out than has been included. For every person whose story is told in these pages, dozens of equally worthy and significant Queen's people have gone unnoted. For every event recalled, innumerable others have been passed by, because with limited text, this book has attempted to reach beyond the core administrative history of the University. Hilda Neatby and Frederick W. Gibson have already written the history of Queen's, and indeed, their work was an invaluable resource in the preparation of this volume. It served as the authoritative source on all matters of fact and was often used to adjudicate among numerous conflicting versions of a given tale, an important task in the history of a university where the various sides of conflicting reports, although often lacking in detail, are always recorded with apparent academic precision and with all the confidence of articulate and highly educated writers.

In *Queen's: The First One Hundred & Fifty Years*, the tale of the University's growth and progress has been supplemented with the spice of its past controversies, with campus myths and legends, even with a couple of the more enduring apocryphal stories. The voice, subject, length and detail of the stories all vary. The smallest anecdotes sometimes receive the same attention as the biographies of influential Principals, and often the footnote to history has been set down rather than the history itself. This book places the accent on different syllables in the story of Queen's and, in words and photographs, offers an imperfect, albeit colourful, reflection of its traditions.

Leonard Brockington, the famous orator and Rector of Queen's University from 1947 to 1966, describing the long and often difficult progress of Queen's, claimed that "the history of this University is the story of a fire that would not be quenched." After 150 years, Brockington's flame still lives, and this book celebrates the countless people who have fuelled the flame and who keep it burning today for the generations of students to come.

Queen's campus, 1919

Looking up past the terrace, Douglas Library

"It is hereby publicly intimated that the first Session of Queen's College, Kingston, will be opened on the first Monday of March next and that then the Professors who have been appointed will begin to teach classes for the following branches of Study: Latin and Greek, Mathematics and Natural Philosophy, Logic and Moral Philosophy, Theology, Church History and Oriental Languages.

"It is particularly requested that those who, for some time past, may have been expecting, according to previous announcements, an earlier opening of the first Session, and which has been prevented by circumstances over which neither the Trustees nor the Professors have had any control, will lose no time after the appearance of this advertisement, in intimating their intention to enrol themselves as Students. Communications from Students or their friends, as to enrolment, may be made either personally or in writing, previous to the day of commencement to Alexander Pringle, Esq., Secretary of the Trustees of Queen's College, Kingston, who will also give information as to the probable duration of the first Session of the College."

— Announcement by Principal Thomas Liddell, January 5, 1842

In the Reign of Victoria

Queen Victoria was in the early years of her reign when the Presbyterians of Canada West finally received the Royal Charter for their College at Kingston. Canada was not yet a nation, and Kingston was not the Limestone City — in 1841, a raging fire destroyed many of the wooden structures that were eventually replaced with stone. British forces were at war in Afghanistan and had proclaimed sovereignty over Hong Kong. American author Edgar Allan Poe had just published *Tales of the Grotesque and Arabesque*. The saxophone was invented by a Belgian named Adolphe Sax. The first year of classes at Queen's, 1842, was also the year the first operation using an anaesthetic was performed. The great British philosopher and political economist John Stuart Mill was at work on his first major work, *A System of Logic*. The world had neither seen the wonders of Samuel Morse's telegraph nor heard of the Brontës — both *Wuthering Heights* and *Jane Eyre* were five years in the future. The planet Neptune was uncharted, and the *Communist Manifesto* was as yet unpublished. Japan still maintained perfect isolation, refusing trade or interaction of any kind with foreigners. And although it may not have been the rage among the young men who presented themselves for education at the new College at Kingston in 1842, the polka was about to make its entry into popular culture.

Queen's early buildings evoke visions of Oxford, Cambridge and Edinburgh universities

Limestone reflected long-term plans

"The College was opened at an abnormal season — in the month of March. There was no navigation and no sleighing. Along with two fellow students, the late John McKinnon, Minister at Carleton Place, and the late Lachlan McPherson, Minister at East Williams, I was driven by a friend from West Flamboro' on Saturday afternoon and drove to Esquesing, where we spent the Sabbath at the home of one of my fellow students. On Monday, we drove to Toronto. In four days, we drove from Toronto to Kingston, reaching the city on Friday night. This was done with the same pair of horses all through; and I doubt if many of our roadsters could do much better now than did that little team, which trotted away merrily home again, arriving in the end of the following week.

"On Saturday morning, we awoke refreshed, with nothing of the sensation of weariness, such as some of us would have now after a drive like that which we had. But we were strangers in the city — a busy place then, being the seat of government in those days. None of the people in the hotel at which we had put up could tell us anything about Queen's College. They had never heard the name. We set out, however, to reconnoitre, although not knowing whither to direct our steps. Reaching the marketplace, a name upon a sign, 'Donald Christie,' caught our eyes. One of us said: 'If there is a Presbyterian college here, a man with a name like that should know something about it.' But, strange to say, although a member of St. Andrew's Church and pleasantly willing to give us any information in his power, he could tell us nothing about the College. Bethinking himself, however, he said, 'Go to the courthouse, ask there for Mr. Pringle, and if there is to be a Presbyterian college opened, he will be able to tell you all about it.' So really we found him to be, and not only so, but before night, he had us all comfortably settled in the snug cottage in which he himself then lived. The following day, we heard Mr. [afterwards the Reverend] Machar in the forenoon and afternoon. None of the students of the time are likely ever to forget the ability and affectionate faithfulness of his ministrations."

— Reverend Thomas Wardrope

Thomas Liddell (1841-46): A Foundering Father

Nominated by the Committee of the General Assembly of the Church of Scotland as the first Principal of Queen's College, Reverend Thomas Liddell arrived in Kingston, Canada West, expecting to assume his position at the head of an institution dedicated to the wisdom of the ages and to the education of thoughtful young Presbyterian ministers. He was expecting to find a university. Instead, he found a group of formidable Scottish pioneers who possessed little else but a Royal Charter — delivered by Liddell himself — an ambitious idea and an abundance of rather stern enthusiasm. The home of the proposed College proved to be no more than a very small town marking the intersection of Lake Ontario and the St. Lawrence and Cataraqui rivers, and to make matters worse, half of the town's buildings had burned to the ground only months before Liddell's arrival.

Rather than teaching young candidates, Liddell was forced to go looking for them. More comfortable with scholarship than with action, Liddell nevertheless spent his first months navigating the countryside's rough roads and canvassing the Presbyterian parishes for both funds and students.

Liddell opened the College in a modest frame house on Colborne Street on March 7, 1842, with a handful of students in attendance and only Professor Peter Colin Campbell to assist him. Yet even then, he got no rest. Instead of finding the uninterrupted freedom to teach his Hebrew and divinity classes, Liddell was drawn further into the controversy over university federation. Seeing it as the only hope for small institutions like Queen's, he wholeheartedly supported the plan to assure secure funding by merging with Toronto's King's College, Victoria College in Cobourg and Kingston's Regiopolis College. He watched with deepening frustration as all attempts at union failed and as legislation designed to bring the schools together was defeated. To add to his difficulty, the split in the Church in Scotland crossed the ocean in 1844, and although Reverend Liddell preached against secession, his sermons, lacking in eloquence and "especially noted for their length," apparently had little effect. By the time the sectarian smoke had cleared, one-third of Queen's students and no fewer than 10 of the College's Trustees had defected. The enrolment in Liddell's divinity class had dropped to one. On July 13, 1846, Queen's first Principal tendered his resignation and, shortly thereafter, departed for Scotland.

"The ship is on the rocks."

— Reverend Robert McGill, Queen's College Trustee, 1846

Upon his arrival in Kingston, Reverend Thomas Liddell delivered the Queen's Royal Charter to the Chairman of the Board of Trustees and presented a letter from the College agent in Edinburgh. Its wording seems, in hindsight, blackly humorous: "I send the present [note] by the Reverend Principal Liddell, to whose care I have committed the Charter of Queen's College, and I sincerely hope that both Principal and Charter may reach Kingston in safety; to protect the College from loss, I shall, however, insure the latter." Charters were expensive — £700 — but Principals were, apparently, not entirely essential. In retrospect, the wording also seems prophetic. From Principal Liddell's resignation in 1846 until Principal William Leitch's appointment in 1859, Queen's College was without an official Principal. For several years, the Trustees continued to hope that Liddell would return, although that fond desire was hardly unanimous. Professor James Williamson's father-in-law wrote from Scotland: "He was most unfitted for communicating instruction to young men — his manner was cold and rigid and formal. I knew nothing about his classical attainments, but he was the most illogical preacher I had ever heard — he had no conclusions, turning round and round in an endless circle . . . if I were him, I would be ashamed to return after the way he had treated the Trustees, and if I were one of them, I would not have him though he were willing to come back."

Williamson's father-in-law need not have worried. Liddell did not return. The Trustees made a formal request in 1849 that Liddell resume his duties as Principal, and he accepted. He sent word that he would return in October of that year, but by March 1850, he had written asking to be withdrawn from "official connexion with Queen's College."

The fact that the College had no Principal caused some confusion for the editors of the "Directory for the City of Kingston" in 1857. "University of Queen's College" is the first entry under the heading Educational Institutions, but the list of professors begins with "Rev._____, Principal and Primarius Professor of Theology."

Mixing Truth With Error

Queen's University at Kingston would have been made a college of a university based in Toronto if Reverend Thomas Liddell, its first Principal, had succeeded in his ambitions. Bishop John Strachan of Toronto, however, viewed the plan as a "measure obnoxious to every right principle, human and divine, offensive to conscience and social order, and such as cannot be entertained for a moment by a Christian nation." Liddell was a Presbyterian, Strachan an Anglican. Both universities prepared young men for their respective ministries, and to mix them together was, in Strachan's mind, to mix truth with error.

An enlightened man, Liddell suggested providing Arts courses for everyone who wanted to attend his proposed federated university. Religious training would be confined to the individual institutions: Regiopolis College, the Roman Catholic School at Kingston; Queen's, the Presbyterian College; Victoria College, the Methodist College headed by the famous Reverend Egerton Ryerson at Cobourg; and the Anglican King's College at Toronto. Liddell was opposed by Strachan, a former Presbyterian, as well as by many others, at every step.

At the heart of the debate that raged throughout the 1840s lay something far more compelling than mere religious bigotry: money. The Anglicans controlled an educational endowment of 250,000 acres of land with an annual income of £12,000 to £15,000, and Liddell, who was forced to raise his funds by travelling around the countryside canvassing local parishes, needed a portion of it. Simply put, Strachan did not want to share.

Southern exposure, Ontario Hall

The idea of a single federated university, situated in Toronto, that would absorb the other colleges of Canada West preoccupied the colony's educators in the mid-19th century. Even after Confederation, the question of efficiency and public funding for education, in one guise or another, remained for some time a threat to the existence of Queen's at Kingston. From the time of his installation as Principal of Queen's in 1877, George Monro Grant took a firm stand on the matter of independent colleges and set an example that helped determine the course of education in Ontario. "There are some things," he wrote, "which really must be considered settled — the creation of the world, the union of the 13 American colonies, the Confederation of Canada and the position of Queen's at Kingston."

By the mid-1880s, Queen's had decisively rejected the idea of joining a provincewide federated university at Toronto. Nonetheless, the question of government support for education remained unresolved. Following Confederation, Ontario had refused to secure the financial position of colleges, and over the years, the debate about money had escalated into a greater controversy about the morality of public funding for religious institutions. The eventual separation of Queen's from the Presbyterian Church — and nearly every other aspect of the College's history — reflected that financial uncertainty and the ongoing need of the College to win government support. "Queen's roots are in the ground, not in the air," wrote George Monro Grant, "and . . . to move her would be to sever her from traditions, associations and affections, the very source of her growth and life."

"Like our fathers, we are willing to cultivate learning on a little oatmeal."

— George Monro Grant

In the mid-19th century, £300 per year seemed a reasonable salary to offer a prospective professor. And there was an extra £100 per annum for the Principal, who would come out from Scotland and lead the new College. In return for this lordly sum, however, the founders of Queen's College had emphatic ideas about what sort of people they wanted. "Not literary and classical drones . . . if they send us out dull men, however prodigious their learning, we are undone," said Reverend Robert McGill. The more spiritual Reverend William Rintoul hoped for "men of deep piety, thorough scholarship, enlarged understanding and acceptable manners." And the ever expedient William Morris, first Chairman of the Board of Trustees, wanted "a practical man of celebrity and experience from one of our Scottish universities. . . . The kind of persons we require are . . . experienced, practical teachers whose duty it will be to educate the pupils before they are qualified to receive lectures from anybody."

Reverend James Williamson somehow proved to be exactly what was required, and much more besides. Principal George Monro Grant's description years later was of "a saint, apostolic . . . not mediaeval, sane, not hysterical." As a professor of mathematics, natural philosophy and astronomy, Williamson helped to transform the tiny denominational College into a small Arts College. Although neither a brilliant scientist nor a great teacher, he inspired an essential dedication and loyalty in students, sentiments he repaid wholeheartedly. Beginning in 1842, he served for over 50 years as a professor, a Trustee and a fund raiser; he was Vice-Principal from 1876 until his death in 1895. During lean times, when some Trustees were eager to abandon the College's commitment to teaching Arts courses, only Williamson's dogged presence and dedication held them off. The Trustees' consciences would not allow them to fire him, and as long as he continued to teach his mathematics and sciences — he seems to have taught every one of the modern sciences to enthusiastic students at one time or another — Queen's remained not only a denominational school but a university as well.

James Williamson, professor, 1842-95

The Domesday Book

Often, the roots of tradition at Queen's University are buried deep in even older lore and rituals. *The Domesday Book of Queen's University* is a handwritten record of Queen's history and benefactors that was patterned on the famous "Domesday Book" of William the Conqueror, a record of all English landowners, their estates and their chattels.

Chancellor Sandford Fleming first proposed *The Domesday Book* in 1888, suggesting that everyone who had contributed to that year's endowment campaign should have his or her name recorded and that a list of all previous patrons should also be included. It was further decided that significant events in the College's history should be set down for posterity. Reverend James Williamson, a longtime staff member, was asked to research and transcribe more than 40 years of the institution's history. Following Williamson's death in 1895, the research was taken over by Lois Saunders, Queen's first full-time librarian. Volume 1 covers the origin of the College until the turn of the century. Volume 2, prepared by Professor Malcolm Macgillivray, covers 1901-24. From that point on, a yearly record of life at Queen's was kept in the annual Principal's Report.

The design and the flowing handwritten script of the earliest pages of *The Domesday Book* were the work of Toshi Ikehara, a young Japanese man who met Principal George Monro Grant during an ocean crossing. That fortuitous meeting eventually brought Ikehara to Kingston, where he became an Arts student in the Class of 1896 and won wide popularity and election to numerous campus offices, including that of secretary of the Alma Mater Society.

Reading Room window, Douglas Library

Ivy-covered wall, Grant Hall

''As a class, medical men have ever
been distinguished by their heroic
self-sacrifice . . . ''

— William Leitch, Inaugural Address, 1860

William Leitch (1859-64): Principal in Absentia

Reverend William Leitch was appointed Principal in 1859, when Queen's College boasted only a handful of students and a 27-member Board of Trustees that outnumbered the staff by more than two to one. Not only did Leitch inherit an unwieldy and top-heavy institution, but he had the misfortune of coming to the task after the College had been without a full-time Principal for more than a decade. His predecessors, the Reverends John Cook and John Machar, had each insisted on temporary appointments as Acting Principal; neither had given up his parish. During the years without leadership, lines of authority had snapped, grievances had festered, and chaos had threatened in those areas where it did not already reign. Little wonder, then, that history records Leitch's tenure as Principal of Queen's as a time of unprecedented scandal and confusion.

The widowed father of two boys, Leitch never did actually take up permanent residence in Kingston. Instead, he returned to Scotland each summer to be with his sons and, one suspects, to recover from the administrative upheavals at Queen's. The practice, however restful it may have been, did little to inspire the confidence of the students and staff under his authority. Without their support, Leitch was slowly overwhelmed by the unchecked agitations of men like Dr. John Stewart of the medical school, who held strong opinions on most subjects and owned a small newspaper, the *Argus*, in which to voice them. At one point, Stewart referred to Leitch in print as a "bungling arch-blockhead."

More serious than Stewart's animosity, however, was the ongoing feud between another two members of the Queen's faculty. Vice-Principal James George and Professor George Weir already shared an intense dislike for one another and a history of enmity when Principal Leitch arrived at Queen's. Two years later, in 1861, this simmering tension came to a rapid boil. Over the summer, Weir learned that his unmarried sister in Scotland was the mother of a 6-year-old son who had been conceived during the time she had shared his house in Kingston. She named James George as the father. In the household of a Scottish Presbyterian minister, an illegitimate child represented an unparallelled disgrace. By the same token, the charge that George, an elder clergyman, had seduced the sister of a colleague could not have been more serious. George denied everything, calling the whole affair a "hellish plot," but he resigned from the College nonetheless. Weir and his wife continued to make accusations and even enlisted the sympathies of students in their battle, at which point the Board of Trustees entered the fray and admonished Weir for allowing "personal feeling to prevail over concern for College discipline."

In the next couple of years, further controversies erupted. Arrangements were made for the College-run preparatory school to merge with the Kingston Grammar School. There was conflict over who would be in charge of the new institution, and an even more divisive fight took place over the establishment of rules, rights and regulations governing the College and its Senate and Board of Trustees. Once again, confusion prevailed. As a group, the professors opposed at least two suggested statutes, which gave to the Trustees power to dismiss any Queen's employee. Debate raged for more than a year, at which point a popular and promising young professor named George Lawson resigned in protest. His farewell meeting in Convocation Hall collapsed into anarchy, and Weir, who was accused of instigating the riotous demonstration, was dismissed at the next Board meeting. Before the dust settled, another professor, John Dickson, had also resigned in protest against the Board's behaviour.

Never having had much of an opportunity to introduce peace and progress at Queen's, William Leitch died in Kingston in May 1864. Strong-willed men with firm convictions had been tending their own affairs at the College for too long, and without a Principal in place, men such as Stewart and Weir had grown used to making their own decisions. Predictably, there was widespread discontent when a leader was introduced for essentially the first time in the institution's nearly 20-year history. It was a testament to his forbearance that Leitch did not resign in frustration during his short, tumultuous career at Queen's.

The First Degree

On June 2, 1847, the first students received their degrees from Queen's College. It was a proud occasion, with Queen's first Senate solemnly awarding certificates of academic achievement. Among these early graduates was Reverend George Bell who, as it turned out, had already embarked upon his own career of firsts at Queen's. His name is the first entered on the roll of Queen's College at its opening. He was also among the founding members of the Dialectic Society of Queen's College, which later became the Alma Mater Society. He was the first and sometimes only student in Principal Thomas Liddell's divinity class. In 1872, Bell became one of the first two alumni to receive an honorary doctorate from Queen's in recognition of his years of service to the Church and to Queen's, as a Trustee. In September 1881, Reverend Bell became Queen's first official Registrar, a post that had previously been the part-time responsibility of John Mowat, professor of Hebrew; from 1883 to 1888, Bell also served as the College's first librarian. Remembered by the student newspaper as "a man of gentlemanly instincts, of amiable, peaceable disposition, genial, gentle bearing, a faithful, painstaking accurate toiler and a scholar," Bell retired in 1897 at the age of 77.

Convocation; spring 1967

Convocation; spring 1990

Since 1854, Summerhill has served, at various times, as a residence, medical school, gymnasium, laboratory and library

In a colony where the Church of England still had a powerful influence on worldly and spiritual matters, many who helped establish Queen's College looked to their new institution as a means of dispelling the lingering impression that Scottish Presbyterians were second-class citizens. For that reason, there was sweet irony in the fact that Summerhill, the College's first permanent home, was purchased in 1854 from a high-ranking Anglican cleric. The streets bordering the onetime Presbyterian denominational College still commemorate Summerhill's previous tenant by using all his names and titles: Arch, Deacon, George, Okill and Stuart.

Among the trees and limestone buildings that have risen around it, Summerhill has itself become a beautiful prospect. Yet it was the view from the archdeacon's home that originally determined its location. At the crest of a gently rising slope, Summerhill commanded an uninterrupted view of both Lake Ontario, stretching away to the western horizon, and the green wooded islands to the south. A stream ran through the grounds, but in later years, it was covered over with boards and buried. And although some people objected that the building was rather far from town, the dramatic style of its construction — the sweeping stairways and pillared porticoes leading to wings at either end — lent it the majesty and authority appropriate to a College building.

The Trustees fancied that their spacious new home, complete with its wood-burning stoves for heat, would serve the young College adequately for a long time. In the space of only a few years, however, the mansion on the hill overflowed with students. As Queen's College began expanding, Summerhill, serving a variety of purposes, always took up the slack. At different times, it has housed students, professors, classrooms, laboratories, the medical school and a gymnasium of sorts. It has even contained the College's library, which dispensed the requested books through an outside window.

A designated Ontario historic site, Summerhill was given a dramatic face-lift in 1984. It continues in its long-standing role as the Principal's official residence — the east wing is reserved for that use — and the Alumni Association now has its home in Summerhill, the oldest building on the Queen's campus.

"A silvery brook . . . meanders merrily . . . across the property — in spring, oft-times a boiling torrent, in summer, a single thread."
— *Queen's College Journal*, 1874

Queen's University was born of a desire for a College in which to educate Presbyterian ministers, and save for the efforts of William Morris, it might well have been limited to that task alone. A successful businessman who helped found the town of Perth, Ontario, Morris was a staunchly honourable man who began his own career by paying off the debts acquired by his father through the disastrous loss of an uninsured ship.

Though intensely practical, Morris was also a visionary, and his principles included powerful convictions about the need for widespread education to improve the lot of his fellow colonial Presbyterians. As the foremost Presbyterian layman in the parliament of Upper Canada, he played a pivotal role in drafting and pushing through the legislation necessary to incorporate a College at Kingston. When that influence gained him the position of Chairman of the Board of Trustees, he fought tooth and nail to limit both the number of clergy on the Board and their influence on the young school. Morris was determined that Queen's should aspire to the status of a university, and his determination helped to sustain Queen's during those years when many supporters considered such ambitions preposterous.

The title of the first draft for an Act of Incorporation referred only to "a College in connexion with the Church of Scotland." Within the text of that May 1, 1839, document, the would-be founders of the proposed institution named it "St. Andrew's College of Canada," in honour of the Scottish institution they so admired.

The Presbyterian Synod, meeting in Kingston in June 1839 to discuss this same College, referred to it as "The Scottish Presbyterian College."

By December 1839, a bill had come before the Legislative Council regarding an institution now to be named "The University of Queen's College at Kingston." Victoria had been Queen since 1837, so the new Royal title lent a certain weight and legitimacy to the endeavour, placing the school ahead of its rival institution, the proposed King's College in Toronto.

After the Governor General pointed out the impropriety of using a Royal title without prior Royal assent, the bill before the parliament of Upper Canada called the institution simply "The University at Kingston."

Only after the legislation was formally disallowed and replaced by Royal Charter — since a Charter, of course, "could not be superinduced upon" — was the name finally settled upon. After listing the original Trustees and professors, the Charter of October 16, 1841, stated that they "shall be and be called, one body Corporate and Politic, in Deed and in Law by the name and style of 'Queen's College at Kingston.'

"We do, for the purposes aforesaid and hereinafter mentioned, really and fully for Us, Our Heirs and Successors, make, erect, create, ordain, constitute, establish, confirm and declare by these present, to be one Body Politic and Corporate in Deed and in name: And that they and their Successors by that name shall and may have perpetual succession as a College — with the style and privileges of an University . . . for the education and instruction of Youth and Students . . . ."

The Ellerbeck Estate

The terms of Act No. 1261 of the legislature of Upper Canada proposing the establishment of a College at Kingston — and later the terms of the Royal Charter itself — required that the College must "not be more than three miles distant from St. Andrews Church [at the corner of Princess and Clergy streets], in the Town of Kingston in the Province of Upper Canada."

Many of the founders' original plans showed truly grand ambition, and the clearest evidence of their heroic intentions was the purchase of the so-called Ellerbeck estate in the early 1840s. At a time when the College could afford to rent only a small single dwelling for its campus on Colborne Street, the Trustees nonetheless purchased 50 acres of land "to the west of Kingston" (in the area between Main Campus and West Campus). The land was located near "Alwington," the proposed Governor General's residence, and indignant Trustees protested strenuously when the price rose from £1,000 to £1,100 due to the land speculation which resulted from the rumour that Kingston would be the capital of the combined Canadas. The same Trustees had, of course, planned some speculation of their own, hoping to take advantage of the town's new status by selling off plots at an inflated price to defray the cost of developing the College property. Indeed, in the years that followed, the land was sold off piecemeal and was often the source of desperately needed funds.

Queen's first classes were held in a rented house on Colborne Street

In the three years that he lived in Kingston, architect George Browne was responsible for building many of the city's most memorable landmarks, including City Hall, St. Andrew's Manse, the Bank of Montreal at the corner of William and King streets, the Rockwood Villa, the Commercial Mart (in later years, the S&R Department Store) and the Wilson's Buildings, on the northwest corner of Wellington and Brock streets. Purchasing an undeveloped plot of land on William Street — "delightfully situated, commanding a charming view of the lake, Long Island, Garden Island, Fort Henry" — Browne also built a home for himself and his new wife. In fact, he constructed two semidetached homes.

But in 1844, after the capital of the combined Canadas moved from Kingston to Montreal, the 33-year-old Browne, who served as official government architect, followed. His houses, complete with the advertised hydraulic pump, patent water closet and cast-iron fireplaces, were put up for rent, and Queen's College and Preparatory School, which had formerly occupied premises on Colborne Street and on Princess Street, opposite St. Andrew's Presbyterian Church, moved in.

Queen's leased additional classroom space on William Street in 1847 and, over the next decade, outlasted several different owners and survived a fire in February 1849. One of the two halves of the building was rented to Professor George Romanes, while the other half housed out-of-town students. A few rules governed these close living and working arrangements, and along with the compulsory classes, students were required to attend church and daily prayers and were forbidden to use profane language or to keep gunpowder and firearms, "ardent spirits" or tobacco. Under no circumstances were they allowed to engage in wrestling. "Pelting with snowballs" was forbidden, as was "getting in and out of the College buildings by other than the ordinary mode of ingress and egress."

In July 1853, the Queen's Trustees determined to replace the George Browne campus on William Street and opened negotiations for the purchase of Summerhill.

Ceilidh, "the central meeting place," John Deutsch University Centre

The imposing stone and ivy walls of Ontario Hall, built 1903

1877-1879, Reverend John Cook
1880-1915, Sir Sandford Fleming
1915-1918, James Douglas
1918-1923, Sir Edward Beatty
1924-1929, Sir Robert Laird Borden
1929-1939, James Armstrong Richardson
1940-1958, The Honourable Charles Avery Dunning
1960-1974, John Bertram Stirling
1974-1980, The Right Honourable Roland Michener
1980-   , Agnes McCausland Benidickson

Among the founders of Queen's College, Reverend John Cook was chosen as the original acting head of the College. Thus he qualifies as the first, albeit temporary, Principal, predating even Reverend Thomas Liddell. In 1857, long after Liddell's departure and the part-time principalship of Reverend John Machar, Cook became Acting Principal for a second time. Twenty years later — by then, one of only four surviving founders and the Moderator of the newly united Presbyterian Church of Canada — he was named the first Chancellor, an office he occupied from 1877 to 1879.

The Chancellor holds the highest official post in the University's complex hierarchy, presiding over convocations and chairing the annual meetings of the University Council. Although the position is largely ceremonial — William Lawson Grant claimed that the title required someone "with the ability to be decorative and dignified" — the Chancellor also serves as an ex officio voting member of the Board of Trustees. Beyond such formal powers, the chancellorship is invariably filled by a person of surpassing accomplishment and national prominence.

John Cook, First Chancellor, 1877-79

After the years of demoralizing squabbles under Principal William Leitch, Reverend William Snodgrass restored a sense of dignity to Queen's College simply by moving his family into Summerhill in 1867 and, for the first time, establishing the Principal's residence on campus.

Snodgrass's time at Queen's churned with Church-related controversy, and as the head of a Presbyterian institution, he often found himself in the middle of the debate. He fought a losing battle for the continuation of government funding for schools, such as Queen's, with strong denominational ties. In the 1860s, negotiations over the reunion of Presbyterian churches raised serious questions about the need for a small college halfway between Montreal and Toronto, and the advantages of shutting down the theology school and finding a place for its Principal in one of the other Presbyterian colleges were discussed at length. Snodgrass fought for the preservation of the school, contributing his own support for the whole process of Presbyterian reunion.

Snodgrass also engineered an endowment campaign from 1869 to 1872 that saved Queen's from bankruptcy after the simultaneous failure of the Commercial Bank, which held a significant portion of the College's capital, and the discontinuation of government support following Confederation. With Professor John Hugh MacKerras, he canvassed from Montreal to Niagara, in many areas visiting not just every parish but often every family within the parish. So pressing was the need and so persuasive was Principal Snodgrass that the residents of Kingston alone donated more than $15,000. Members of the faculty handed back as much as one-third of their salaries. In the end, the goal of $100,000 was not only met but surpassed.

Eventually, however, Snodgrass grew weary of the battles that relentlessly came his way. Instead of being free to teach and study and oversee the steady advance of the school, his energies were sapped by the need to fight against the rearguard actions threatening the very existence of Queen's. When the Reverend D.J. Macdonnell heresy scandal rocked the Church and brought charges that Queen's encouraged impiety, Snodgrass had already contemplated retirement. (Macdonnell's sin? He had questioned the belief of many Presbyterians that eternal punishment awaited those who died unconverted.) Snodgrass's defence of Macdonnell, a graduate of Queen's, before the Church assembly marked Snodgrass's eloquent and dignified withdrawal from the College's affairs. An offer, in 1877, of the parish of Canonbie in Scotland proved too tempting; that fall, Snodgrass tendered his resignation.

The Trustees were caught unaware by Snodgrass's abrupt decision to leave Queen's. They ungraciously noted his departure in the minutes, offering no more than a stilted acknowledgment of appreciation and withholding the six months' pay that was due Snodgrass upon his departure. Although he never forgave the slight nor contributed another penny to Queen's, Snodgrass performed one last act that served to transform Queen's into a major educational institution: he recommended George Monro Grant as his successor.

"Queen's has a potent and mysterious spell . . . . Her very dust to me is dear."

— William Snodgrass to George Monro Grant

The Martyr of Queen's

Often described as the martyr of Queen's, John Hugh MacKerras worked himself literally to death during the endowment campaigns mounted by Principals Snodgrass and Grant. Long, hard days of travel and an endless schedule of meetings, appointments and visits eventually broke the health of Professor MacKerras. The task of calling on every potential supporter of Queen's — in the cities and deep in the countryside — proved too much, and he died in January 1880, after a holiday in the south of France had failed to restore his health.

Yet MacKerras may be remembered also as an example of the kind of professor who carried Queen's through its first tremulous decades. He was not a world-ranked scholar with a conspicuous list of credentials but, rather, a man who had been raised in the tiny town of Lyn, Ontario, and had acquired an impressive education that he was determined to pass on to others. A graduate of Queen's, MacKerras was a Presbyterian minister but was also qualified to teach the classics and was fluent in both French and Italian. Remembered by his students as a paragon of professorial virtues, he was kind, patient, fair and dedicated.

Summerhill became home to its first Principal in 1867

The minutes of the University Senate for January 12, 1858, describe a letter signed by several students "craving the countenance and support of the Senatus in favour of a Society about to be formed by them in connection with Queen's College, the objects of which Society are — maintenance and defence of students' rights, the interchange of friendly intercourse, the promotion and encouragement of learning and the furtherance of the general interests of the University." The Senate gave its wholehearted approval, and the Alma Mater Society (AMS), first known as the Dialectic Society of Queen's College, was born.

The early AMS pursued one of its original mandates: "to cultivate a literary and scientific taste among the students." Fortnightly meetings were given over to the consideration of such esoteric topics as "the fate of Mary, Queen of Scots, the character of Oliver Cromwell and the relative merits of the contributions of the English and the Scots to literature." By 1908, on-campus elections had become highly politicized, a reflection of the AMS's increasing role in governing students' nonacademic affairs. From the time of Principal George Monro Grant onward, in fact, University authorities had seen the wisdom of avoiding confrontation by urging students to take care of their own business, and out of a frontier spirit of independence came the Queen's students' highly prized tradition of self-government.

The modern AMS would astound its founding members. In its contemporary form, the student regime handles a staggering array of tasks and is composed of a voting assembly of almost 50 members headed by a three-person executive — President, Vice-President, Operations, and Vice-President, University Affairs. This body meets every two weeks and hears motions raised by any student of the University. Like any government, the AMS includes a police force in the form of the Queen's Student Constables, who supervise student (and alumni) conduct at football games and at other large Queen's gatherings. And the AMS has a sizable bureaucracy, including dozens of standing committees administered by five commissions, each with an appointed commissioner: Campus Activities, Communications, Education, External Affairs and Internal Affairs. In addition, the AMS has a Services Director and a Publications Director, areas of responsibility that include campus pubs, convocation hood-and-gown rentals, a bus service, an entertainment agency, the *Queen's Journal* and the *Tricolour* yearbook.

Witness for the defence; AMS Court, 1924

The AMS Court began — on sunny afternoons behind the breweries of Kingston — as an entirely informal operation. The Court was started by upper-year students who supplemented their drinking funds by seizing freshmen, charging them with manufactured crimes, trying them before the Court and promptly finding them guilty. Witnesses swore on a dictionary in the name of the janitor. Fines were levied and immediately used to buy more refreshments, and if the "criminal" was a good sport, he was invited to join in the drinking.

As years went by, the Court evolved into a more formal body regulating such lofty matters as dress codes and hat-wearing privileges, but archival photographic evidence suggests that the self-styled *Concursus iniquitatis et virtutis* still resisted all pressures to take itself entirely seriously. In the latter two decades of the 19th century, the Court seemingly spent most of its energy dressing up each year and posing for the camera in smirking group settings complete with judge, prosecutor, defence attorney, bailiff, witnesses and the condemned criminal, hooded and bent beneath the impending blow of a gruesome, bloody broadaxe.

As the AMS accepted its growing role as a governing body on campus, the Court, too, took on sterner tasks. Both institutions earned Principal George Monro Grant's support, and under his influence, the Court gradually gave up its commitment to frivolity. It became instead a defender of tradition and convention and, in time, adopted a formal and more serious tone.

Along with maturity, the years of dispensing student justice have also brought occasional charges of humourless self-seriousness. In 1957, the Court fined nine women students — "the naughty nine" — $10 each and sentenced them to 10 hours' work for the Levana Society. Their crime? Raiding the men's dormitory at the Royal Military College on Halloween. "We are truly the 'no-nonsense kids,'" observed the *Queen's Journal*, noting that "many people hissed at the sober, heavy judgment."

In its modern guise, the merry court of old has become a Judicial Committee. And while in many respects, the institution is but a dry shadow of its former lusty self, it possesses powers commensurate with its position as a duly constituted arm of the AMS that "seeks to resolve nonacademic disputes and breaches of the Queen's Code of Conduct."

The pantheon of exalted figures at Queen's University boasts no one so great as Reverend George Monro Grant. Between his installation as Principal in 1877 and his death in 1902, he transformed Queen's into a national university. The campus grew, new buildings appeared, enrolment quintupled, and the very atmosphere was informed by a new sense of purpose.

Grant commanded an emotionally charged respect — ''Geordie, our King'' the students called him — and he reciprocated with unstinting dedication. Even in his own time, he achieved near mythic stature.

Yet Grant possessed no magic, simply an unparalleled capacity for work, an eager curiosity about all he saw, a sharp mind and a liberal-hearted wisdom grounded in his abiding Christian faith.

Grant's accomplishments were endless in number and far-reaching in significance. He quashed lingering suggestions that Queen's College become part of the provincial university at Toronto, a dispirited plan that had tempted the College since its beginning. He staked out a place for the small independent university and thus helped determine the course of education in Ontario and in the country as a whole. He brought the estranged medical school back within the College, established the School of Mining and Agriculture and founded the *Queen's Quarterly*. He launched heroic endowment campaigns, fought to acquire government funding and, in the midst of his busiest days, made time for students to come to him with their problems and ideas. Although their numbers grew, he continued to know all the students by name as well as something about their hometowns and family histories.

Grant's clear ideas of where the country should be headed and his equally certain vision of the College's role in that progress lifted Queen's from its uncertain first decades and sent it hurtling into the 20th century.

"Asked if he did not find it difficult to control the youth who poured in annually from the farms and rural villages, full of the New World distrust for authority, he replied: 'We teach them to control themselves.' "
— from *Principal Grant*, by William Lawson Grant and Frederick Hamilton, 1904

"It was a marvel how he kept Queen's financed. It is true that his staff worked for the joy of the working. Their salaries provided for nothing but plain living and were never increased. Fifteen hundred dollars, as I remember, was what the head of a department received, and out of that, Geordie was wont to 'wangle' very substantial contributions to his pet schemes. When a man thought he needed more, Geordie reminded him that when he himself needed fifty dollars, he wrote an article — and he did encourage the staff to supplement their incomes by productive scholarship along saleable lines. He lost one or two otherwise good men on account of the small salary, but he did not waver in his policy. Men of the type he wanted were willing to join such a leader in sacrifice for a great cause; and Geordie knew that loyalty and devotion are born of sacrifice and sustained by it."
— from " 'Geordie': Some Recollections," Part I, by R.W. Brock, *The Queen's Review*, November 1928

Principal George Monro Grant

Some, like John Watson and Nathan Fellowes Dupuis, were at Queen's when Principal George Monro Grant arrived in 1877; and others, Grant invited himself: young professors who were to become well-respected scholars in their fields. Principal Grant impressed upon them the importance of writing and publishing and reaching beyond the school's walls to carve a place for themselves among the world's scholars. And while he applied constant pressure to that end, he also provided endless encouragement. More important, he infused them with the conviction that together, they were building a national university. These were "Grant's Men."

Some of Grant's Men: James Cappon, Nathan Dupuis, John Macnaughton, John Watson

James Cappon, professor of English literature, took his degree from Glasgow University in Scotland. Before arriving at Queen's, however, he had had a teaching appointment in Genoa, Italy, in 1882, where he gained a comprehensive knowledge of Italian literature. Remembered for his aloofness and his reputedly dogmatic ways, he nonetheless won great affection from his students, and it is little wonder. He maintained that "a language is taught not just that it may be spoken but to unlock the treasures of its literature." For 31 years, from 1888 to 1919, he helped generations of students discover those treasures.

A professor of philosophy, John Watson was not entirely certain about Kingston and Queen's when he arrived from Glasgow in 1872. Yet "the whole atmosphere," he observed, "seemed to radiate with life and enthusiasm." He decided to stay. It is well that he did. From this small College in a small town beside Lake Ontario, John Watson ascended to the highest ranks of contemporary scholars, one of the last of the great Christian Idealist philosophers. Professor Watson's lectures transformed philosophy from one of the least popular to one of the best-loved courses on campus.

An unequivocal man, confident in the power of truth and of his own intellect, Watson once observed of himself and his colleagues that "timid people think we are 'dangerous.' I think we are. We are very dangerous to superstition and tradition and intellectual sloth. . . . I venture to say, knowing whereof I speak, that we have saved many young men from shallow skepticism . . . and traditionalism, by treating them as men, not as babes."

If it could be built, Professor Nathan Fellowes Dupuis could build it; if it could be understood, he could tell you the theories behind it. Captivated by the ways and means of the physical world, Dupuis was an astronomer who knew the maps of the heavens by memory — in fact, he began his career as a student at Queen's in 1863 and that same year was appointed an observer at the College's observatory. In 1868, Dupuis became a professor of chemistry and natural history. Acting as a guide to the new ways of science and technology, he introduced the old enclave of the humanities to a new and sometimes contradictory worldview. The evidence of his broad-ranging talents and integrating efforts in all areas of the College emerged at Dupuis' retirement in 1911, when admirers endowed three scholarships in his name — in Arts, Medicine and Science.

Trained at the University of Aberdeen and ordained in the Church of Scotland, Reverend John Macnaughton came to Queen's in 1889 as a professor of Greek. At his installation, he described himself and the world as he saw it with a single, unlikely confession. "I admit Greek is of no use," he said, and has had no "direct practical utility . . . since the fall of the Roman Empire," but "I glory in the uselessness of it . . . as a protest against Philistine utilitarianism." Such a man could not fail to inspire young students.

For five short years, T.R. Glover taught the classics at Queen's before returning to St. John's College, Cambridge, to resume the brilliant career he had begun there as a student. Between 1896 and 1901, he managed to shift the emphasis from the simple teaching of the Latin language to the study of its literature. Hired by Principal George Monro Grant himself and welcomed into the Queen's community, Glover developed a great fondness both for his colleagues and for Queen's. His later writings acknowledged his debt to the Queen's of Grant's day, and he returned regularly to Kingston and to Queen's for the rest of his life.

Accompanied by his parents, young Adam Shortt attended a speech given by Principal Grant at Walkerton, Ontario, in 1878. Afterward, Shortt's mother, inspired by Grant's words, turned to him and said, "We don't know anything about Queen's or what it is like, but wherever that man is, that is where you are going." As historian D.D. Calvin recounts the story told to him by Shortt himself, he did as his mother instructed, although he had every intention of transferring to Toronto after Christmas to attend the school of his choice.

After winning a general scholarship, however, the young student remained, eventually winning the medal for philosophy in his graduating year. After three years of further study at the universities of Glasgow and Edinburgh, he returned to Queen's. From that point on, his interests steadily evolved from philosophy to economics and political science, and eventually, he took a job in government service in Ottawa. Thus Queen's connection to the capital began with one of Grant's Men, who had been wooed to the College by the legendary Principal's oratorical style.

Born out of turmoil, the Queen's medical school remained a centre of controversy for years after it was established. Like the College itself, the medical faculty began as a response to sectarianism. Toronto's Bishop John Strachan had decided that Trinity College would become strictly Anglican, and medical students at Toronto discovered that their degrees would not be conferred unless they were members in good standing of the Anglican Church. Since Queen's policy forbade a religious test for entrance in 1854, nine of the Trinity students petitioned Queen's to establish a medical faculty. In the fall of that year, they joined 14 others in Kingston. Lecturers rather than full professors taught their classes, and the students paid their salaries directly.

Over the next 11 years, the Board of Trustees equivocated about whether or not it wanted the responsibility for the new addition to the College. The medical faculty, for its part, resisted pressure to accept the authority of the Board of Trustees, and a strange arm's-length relationship was consequently maintained. Unresolved questions about money and hierarchy eventually caused an open rift, and in 1866, the medical school split away to form the Royal College of Physicians and Surgeons of Kingston. Technically, however, Queen's continued to confer its degrees, and 14 years later, Principal George Monro Grant tempted the school back onto the campus by offering to rent it the Old Medical Building for $1 per year. But not until 1892 did the Royal College of Physicians and Surgeons once again become Queen's Faculty of Medicine.

The formal definition of medicine's position within Queen's remained unspecified for a decade after Grant's action, but in 1903, Dr. James Cameron Connell was named Dean of the Faculty of Medicine. He quickly proved to be one of those people essential to the history of Queen's; his energy and coherent vision brought lively progress to even the most stagnant situation. Under Connell's supervision, standards were raised, the faculty was properly established, and laboratory work became part of the medical programme. Queen's medicine was placed on the secure footing it has enjoyed ever since.

Not all of the interesting characters who have passed through Queen's University's medical faculty have aided its progress. In fact, the medical school just barely withstood the attentions of one Dr. John Stewart. Recognized for his unflagging professional devotion to his patients, Stewart was, nonetheless, a feisty and irascible individualist whose thundering opinions often appeared in his own newspaper, the *Argus*. After prolonged conflict between Stewart and almost everyone else in sight — a conflict that began when Stewart objected to what appeared to be the patronage appointment in 1860 of a 19-year-old named Alfred Sales Oliver to the position of house surgeon at Kingston General Hospital — the College gave several reasons for Stewart's eventual dismissal in 1862: he had usurped the authority of the Trustees; he had published statements injurious to Queen's; he had insulted his colleagues; and he had neglected his duties. Stewart's response in the *Argus* was to call Principal William Leitch "the head sinner of a degraded Queen's College."

After Stewart's departure, the College was forced to consult its solicitors on how best to recover the skeleton, microscope, embalming instruments and disarticulated head that Stewart had taken with him when he left. The relationship did not improve. When Stewart later found himself jailed for libel and friends circulated a petition to have him released, the Queen's Senate responded by unanimously sponsoring a counterpetition demanding that he be left where he was.

In an essay entitled "Reminiscences of Dr. John Stewart," John Watson illustrates the sharp mixture of wit and temper that so enlivened the early years of Queen's medicine with a story about Stewart's being called as a witness in a trial. "A horse had been accidentally killed by the tram of a lorry," writes Watson. "A little cockney lawyer put to the witness the foolish question, 'Dr. Stewart, did you ever dissect a horse?' 'No,' the exasperated witness replied, 'but if you were dead (sniff), I would damned soon dissect (sniff) an ass.' "

In the early decades of the College's existence, the medical students fancied themselves to be the rougher element of the College population, more in touch with life's realities than were their Arts and Divinity compatriots. The unpleasant necessity of working with cadavers no doubt partly explained that attitude, and the medical students heartily approved of the College song's claim that "They often rob the graves / Of defunct and extinct braves / On the Old Ontario Strand." A.A. Travill in his *Medicine at Queen's, 1854-1920 — A Peculiarly Happy Relationship* suggests that behind the joking, "some evidence of illicit traffic in 'the lately deceased' from Hay Bay to Kingston disguised as shipments of apple barrels does exist." His footnote quotes faculty minutes for April 7, 1903:

"The question of the scandal in connection with the recent attempted grave robbery was discussed, and the whole question of supply of anatomical material was referred to a committee."

Their familiarity with corpses and surgery added to the mystique of medical students

For more than 70 years, the Levana Society, formed in 1888, provided the hub about which the lives of Queen's women students and graduates revolved. Members held meetings, organized tea dances and lectures and sponsored debates on topical questions. They also co-hosted a yearly concert and dance to which members of the Kingston community were invited.

Far more than a mere club, Levana was founded during a period when women still felt themselves to be somehow unofficially on probation within the university community, when women moved quickly and discreetly between classes with eyes cast down lest they draw attention to their presence. The Levana Society provided a refuge from the sense of isolation most women on campus felt, and it "became the common unifying force in the life of Queen's women students." Of course, it was not the perfect solution; an 1891 *Queen's College Journal* report describing a Levana gathering gives voice to the paradoxical ambivalence that enforced self-reliance brought with it: "It was a pity the boys were not there to see how well we could get on without them."

In time, Levana gave real strength to women's voices at Queen's by assuming the role of women's student government and by forming such coalitions as the victorious 1933 Arts-Levana-Theology party in order to influence the Alma Mater Society elections.

On the question of sororities, Levana members had clear opinions. "With one universal organization," argued a submission to the *Queen's Journal* in 1930, "the snobbish cliques, which are so often found elsewhere, are greatly eliminated. It matters not whether your ancestors were United Empire Loyalists, whether your father has retired on a vast income and you drive a Cord or whether you come from some obscure little town and are working your way through. What you yourself are is all that matters."

As women approached an equal footing within the broader community, the perception of a need for a University-wide women's society diminished. Nonetheless, Levana remained a force to be considered and, in 1961, took a lead in circulating a petition protesting a controversial decision to erect a new physics building on the scenic Lower Campus. For generations of Queen's women, however, Levana provided something far more essential than mutual aid and influence: it was a spiritual touchstone and a society of friends.

Orientation, fall 1989

In 1806, German essayist Jean Paul Richter published a treatise proposing dramatic changes to the role of women in society. His reasons may have been slightly pessimistic, yet his exhortation that women cease to belittle their own gender and seize a new role in society strikes a chord today. "It may possibly happen in time," he wrote, "that all the men may be engaged in a war and peace establishment. It seems to me that we should think more of educating girls to be the conductors of our business and the managers of our estates. . . . O, mother, above all other things, implant and cherish in your daughter a love and reverence for her own sex."

To the young women of Queen's in 1888 who had gathered together in sisterhood, these would have seemed the perfect words to shape their paths in a world of change — change already demonstrated by their very presence at a university. Richter called his essay "Levana," and the young late-Victorian women of Queen's took the name for their new organization: Levana — the Roman goddess, the rising sun, sister of dawn, patroness of childbirth, a symbol of renewal.

Of course, even such a lofty beginning has a human side. The name Levana, with Richter's connotations of radical change, came to the students from John Macgillivray, a Queen's professor of languages and a lover of German literature. Macgillivray had been approached for advice because the women were confident of his interest and assistance; he had, after all, a special interest in one of the fledgling members, Annie Campbell of Perth, whom he later married.

Levana executive committee, 1899

The Collector

Many years before he became a professor at Queen's, young William Nicol attended a lecture given by Professor Nathan Fellowes Dupuis at the Cataraqui Town Hall, just west of Kingston. The words of the great man filled the room, and they might have awakened in the boy a fascination with science. Nicol, however, was not listening. Although he later dated his interest in science to that same evening, it was not the talk which inspired him. It was the oxyhydrogen flame used to light the lantern projecting pictures onto a screen at the front of the room. He wanted to know why it burned so brightly.

That curiosity never abated. In due course, Nicol became a student at Queen's, and although he also took awards in Greek, French, rhetoric and English literature, he turned his prodigious talents to the study of chemistry. After postgraduate work in Germany, he returned to Queen's in 1891 as an assistant professor of chemistry. It is a tribute to the respect that Nicol commanded (as well as an indication of the difficulty of finding competent professors) that with the rapid expansion of the Kingston School of Mining and Agriculture in the early 1890s, he was asked to retrain himself in order to teach mineralogy. He agreed, and after further studies in Europe at Freiburg and Heidelberg, he took up his new position in earnest in 1896.

In subsequent years, Professor Nicol acquired two reputations — one as a stern classroom disciplinarian who had little patience for those who did not take the subject seriously; the second as an eager, friendly man who conducted classes in his home and took his students on regular field trips.

Nicol's great passion was the collection of mineral specimens he assembled for Queen's. In an article in a 1929 *Queen's Review,* his colleague E.L. Bruce recounted Nicol's firm belief that a mineral specimen in private hands was never as well cared for and never as useful as it was in a public collection. "Hence," Bruce continued, "he felt that not merely was he justified but that he was to be commended in obtaining an unusual mineral or exceptional crystal by any means at his disposal." No examples of Nicol's methods follow that intriguing statement, however. He kept no samples for himself but, instead, donated them all to Queen's.

With no immediate family, Nicol devoted both his energies and his financial resources to the School of Mining and Agriculture, making many gifts of equipment both to his own department and to others as well. There were discreetly repeated stories of the students he had helped over rough times, and $40,000 of his own money went into the construction of Nicol Hall.

Geology Museum, Miller Hall

Geological field trip, 1945

''Even in Theology, a practical use
can often be made of Geology.''
— *Queen's University Journal*, 1893

After 150 years, Theology operates as a small, independent college affiliated with Queen's University, a college that boasts fewer staff and students than do many of the University's departments. In the beginning, however, the education of ministers was the most important function of the Presbyterian College at Kingston. In fact, Queen's University owes its very existence to the Presbyterian Synod, and it remained associated with the Church and under its guardianship for more than 70 years. During that time, most of the important issues and controversies that shaped the institution were born of its dual ambition to be both a divinity college and a university offering an ever-increasing range of classes to all who wished to study, regardless of their religious affiliation. (The College began its life amidst a debate about the proper balance of clergy and laity on the Board of Trustees.) The first professors were Presbyterian ministers, and every Principal from Liddell to Gordon bore the title "Primarius Professor of Divinity." The first class of 10 matriculated students included theological students as well as young men interested in other disciplines.

As Queen's became increasingly dedicated to teaching the Arts and Sciences in the late 19th and early 20th centuries, the question of whether a theology school and a university did not perhaps represent and pursue different worldviews emerged. Fortunately, the liberal-minded wisdom of such Principals as William Snodgrass, George Monro Grant and Daniel Miner Gordon ensured that the received dogmas of the Church did not stifle scientific inquiry. Similarly, in the years since, the chauvinism of science and technical progress has not been allowed to silence the voice of spirituality at Queen's.

On frequent train trips, Reverend Samuel Walters Dyde liked to spend his time knitting, much to the consternation of less enlightened fellow travellers. These were the days of late Victorian and Edwardian propriety, and men did *not* knit — certainly not in public places. How much more surprised witnesses would have been to learn that this man was also a philosopher, poet, theologian, literary critic, professor and the eminently respectable principal of a school of theology.

Dyde came to Queen's in the early 1880s and retired in 1934. For 22 years, he taught mental philosophy, and after leaving to lead Robertson Theology College in Edmonton for seven years, he returned to head the Queen's Theological College in 1918-19, just as World War I was ending. He was a crusader who believed that Queen's Theology should be a transforming influence on the Presbyterian Church as it met the new challenges of a peacetime world. Dyde viewed parochialism as the fundamental human error and maintained the need for greater understanding among peoples and the corresponding need for Christian unity. His suggestions — for instance, that Queen's Presbyterian Theological College should hire a non-Presbyterian professor — were usually frustrated by more conservative superiors, but history proved that Samuel Dyde had merely been ahead of his time.

Drama students rehearse in the Theological College's original convocation hall

Practical Skills and Timely Gifts

In 1849, when he was 13 years old, Nathan Fellowes Dupuis made a working clock from materials he had gathered on his father's farm. More than half a century later, he built the most famous timepiece on the Queen's University campus. In the years between, he became a scientist, a mathematician and a teacher, playing an important role in the establishment of the Kingston School of Mining and Agriculture (later part of the Faculty of Applied Science). He taught chemistry to medical students, and he actively supported women at Queen's during their very first years, teaching some of the earliest mixed classes and lecturing for the Women's Medical College despite the controversy and opposition which surrounded that institution. After the death of Principal George Monro Grant in 1902, Dupuis served as Acting Principal for several months.

During his long career, Dupuis continued to honour practical skill above all else. Through the many lean years at Queen's, all science equipment used for demonstrations and experimentation as well as mathematical and geometric models were handmade by Dupuis, whose passion for astronomy also led him to create a sophisticated series of clocks, regulators and moving dials designed to show the shifting positions of the planets.

There was very little that Dupuis could not accomplish, and his dedication to the University was unsurpassed. Yet when students approached him for a contribution to the fund to erect a new convocation hall in honour of George Monro Grant, he declined. He could not give money, he said, for he had none. Instead, he offered to design and build a clock to be placed in the tower of the new hall. With the assistance of James C. Connell, an instructor in the Mechanical Laboratory, he created an eight-day movement employing a 13-foot-long pendulum. Holes had to be cut in the floor of the laboratory to allow its construction, and more holes had to be knocked into the side of the tower in order to put the pieces in place. Once it was assembled and its balsa-wood hands affixed, however, it became an instant symbol. Not only a tribute to Grant, the clock was also a conspicuous reminder of the skills Dupuis acquired as a farm boy and sharpened through years of teaching the students of Queen's.

The clock tower, Grant Hall

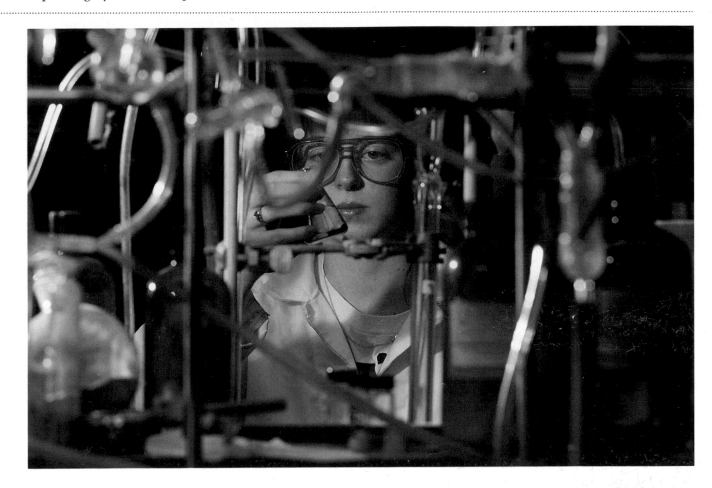

''I will build in my own shop and with my hands and equipment a large clock which can be placed in the hall tower.''
— Professor Nathan Fellowes Dupuis

Some beginnings are humbler than others. Some successes are greater. The history of the department of electrical engineering at Queen's reflects both these claims. Its impressive home in the Technology Centre on Union Street is a symbol of the department's contemporary eminence, and a simple quotation framed and mounted in the main stairwell of the building recalls its modest beginnings.

The quoted text, a course description from the 1894-95 calendar, promises that "a special series of experiments will be conducted for the study of electricity in all its variations of thermo-electricity, voltaic-electricity, magneto-electricity and magnetism, and illustrations will be given, by means of various models and small machines, of this wonderful form of energy to telegraphy, telephony, electric lighting and the driving of machinery."

This 19th-century study plan gives very little indication of the progress to come, both in the world of electricity and at Queen's. The course description does not even mention electrons, and there is not the slightest hint that the department would one day investigate everything from radio waves and the interstellar signals of extraterrestrial bodies to the feasibility of robotic arms with sensing capabilities. In 1894, no one could have imagined an electronic computer; the modern role of anything like a microchip was beyond fantasy.

Yet although Professor L.W. Gill, the first head of electrical engineering, may not have known what he was touching off with his original course outline, the department's mandate was nonetheless boldly set down in that description: "electricity in all its variations."

Beyond imagination: laser technology

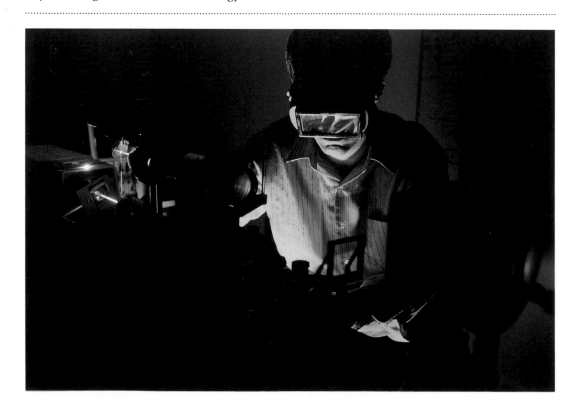

Solar car, electrical/mechanical engineering collaboration, 1989

A 1983 study of space needs across the campus concluded that without question, electrical engineering faced the most critical crowding problem of any department on campus. People described the laboratories as "sweat shops," and demands for space could no longer be met within the buildings of the Fleming quadrangle, the department's traditional home. Additions to the existing structures threatened the prized aesthetics of the campus core, and as well, there seemed some obvious reasons for locating an entirely new building on Union Street next to Goodwin Hall, home of both the department of mining engineering and the department of computing and information science.

Given the often converging interests of computer scientists and electrical engineers, the adjacent buildings on Union Street made good, practical sense. They also offered a symbol of the changing times and the progress made. In fact, the move seemed a natural evolution of the campus; Goodwin Hall even included design features adapted to exactly this kind of expansion. Yet given the financial obstacles, Principal Ronald Watts' decision to go ahead with the Technology Centre represented a leap of fund-raising faith. Committees were formed, plans made and grand schemes begun, but all the activity went ahead without a dollar to back it up.

Such dramatic financial problems often draw equally dramatic financial solutions, and Principal Watts was vindicated — perhaps saved from his own optimism — when a bequest from Joseph S. Stauffer (Science '20) provided a financial foundation for the centre. Dennis Jordan, the executor of the Stauffer estate, approved payment of $2.3 million to Queen's on condition that the Ontario government pledge a matching grant. The Technology Centre was officially opened on March 3, 1989, but not before anonymous donations of over $500,000 made possible the addition of a superb 180-person lecture theatre.

Where Is Frontenac Hall?

Only months after receiving Chancellor Sandford Fleming's request for assistance in funding the construction of a much-needed building in the spring of 1900, the City of Kingston passed a bylaw authorizing the donation of $50,000 to Queen's. Kingston Hall is named after the city whose citizens generously made its existence possible. The response of the citizens of Frontenac County, however, proved to be an entirely different story. When asked to sponsor a convocation hall to be named Frontenac Hall, they took the matter under consideration, and on November 1, 1901, they, too, held a vote. The next day, Dr. Michael Sullivan, a lecturer in surgery at Queen's, had this to say to his class:

"One would have imagined that they would have tumbled over each other in their eagerness to reach the polls and deposit their votes for the bonus. As it was, they went for that poor bonus like a pack of ravenous wolves, tearing it tooth and nail and completely destroying it. Shades of Frontenac and LaSalle, who first set foot on these shores. If that distinguished man after whose name the County is called could hear of it, it would be little wonder if he turned in his grave."

The new convocation hall became known as Grant Hall. Its renaming was tinged with irony. In all likelihood, Frontenac County prohibitionists had helped to block the approval of a donation to Queen's; Principal George Monro Grant had publicly opposed their cause in the national liquor referendum of 1898, and the stern folk of that county clearly held a grudge.

Carved in Stone

In order to contribute to the building fund for what is now called Grant Hall, Queen's students picked berries and donated their wages, raided their bank accounts if they had them and returned scholarships and even salaries paid to them as tutors. Graduating students went forth not only to establish themselves in the world but also to secure income to pay what they had subscribed to the building fund. Some had committed themselves to contribute money for 10 years.

An unmistakable symbol of Queen's since the day it was dedicated, Grant Hall was built as a personal tribute to the best-loved figure in the history of the University. In 1901, even as Frontenac County declined its support, students had initiated the building fund. It was an eager display of affection, and with the suggestion that the hall actually be named for Principal George Monro Grant, the fund-raising campaign became a crusade very close to the heart of virtually everyone associated with Queen's.

Because it was, in the words of J. Lorne MacDougall in the March 1933 *Queen's Review*, "ornamented with the illustrious name of Grant, the man whose heart and intellect had been at once the toughest and most colourful thread in the warp and woof of the Queen's fabric for a quarter of a century, the project was informed with a spiritual power that no friends of Queen's could resist."

Sadly, the tribute became a memorial before the sod was even broken. In May 1902, Grant died after a winter-long illness. But there is a lovely logic to be found in the fact that even in death, as in so much of his life, Principal Grant focused people's attention and resources in a way that brought growth and long-term benefit to Queen's. It is a profound compliment to the man who transformed a small college into a national institution that the profile of the building named for him has become synonymous with Queen's University.

Grant Hall; a student tribute became a memorial to the University's best-loved Principal

"If you build the hall and call it 'Frontenac Hall,' I will donate $100; but if you call it 'Grant Hall,' I will give you $1,000."
— The Honourable William Harty, Board of Trustees of Queen's College, 1902

It has changed in size; it has changed in tone; it has varied in length over the years; and it has changed its name. Nothing about the *Queen's Journal* ever stays the same. Although the students' publication eventually became a newspaper, the original eight-page pamphlet, published on October 25, 1873, had quite different intentions. It sought to "foster a literary taste among the students," and poetry figured prominently in its pages. Since opinions were far more amusing than news, the *Journal* of the 1870s and 1880s kept facts to a minimum, preserving plenty of space for editorializing and for articles on such matters as "How We Should Regard the University" and "The True Student."

The *Queen's College Journal* became the *Queen's University Journal* in March 1893 and simply the *Queen's Journal* in October 1911. By that time, the original tiny booklet had evolved into a full-fledged newspaper that carried headlines and photographs under an impressive banner. In keeping with tradition, the line between information and opinion remained foggy, but increasingly, the *Journal* settled into a happy blend of news, campus events and announcements. Each editor imparted a slightly different style to the *Journal*, and just as the Victorian age lent a certain stuffiness to the first years, the changing times of the 20th century were usually reflected in the selection of stories and in the style of presentation. A careful attention to international news was conspicuous in the postwar 1950s; the 1970s were noteworthy for the introduction of the word "dope" into the *Journal* lexicon.

In 1973, the *Journal* passed its centennial mark and carried on into a second century without breaking stride. Flexibility accounts for its survival, as does the hard work of its ever-changing staff. Yet the *Journal* has done more than merely survive; it has maintained standards, has eschewed gimmicks and, while taking its role on campus seriously, has always earned the proof of its success, a healthy circulation.

"Best Baths in Ontario"

In the pages of the old *Queen's College Journal*, amid articles on such solemn topics as "What Is Preaching?" and "Thomas Carlyle's Wit," the advertisements survive as the true artifacts of a bygone era. They are reminders of the little details that history sometimes ignores, and they describe everything from life's necessities to the idle conceits of earlier generations of students.

Like many researchers, Queen's historian D.D. Calvin knew all about this source of historical trivia, and in his 1941 history of the University, he set down a number of the best advertisements from the early years of the *Journal*. Among his favourites were a barbershop in 1887 promising "Best Baths in Ontario" and a hatter offering "Heads Fitted by a Paris Conformateur." He noted "collars and cuffs in linen and celluloid" and found offers of "oysters — plate, can or quart." He expressed puzzlement over advertisements for mysterious items called "responsible sticks," and in the liveryman's 1889 offer of "hacks — for all trains and to all parts of the city," Calvin caught a glimpse of Kingston before the invention of the automobile.

Of course, other advertisements from those early days catch the eye of a modern reader in ways that Calvin did not see in 1941. Photography, for instance, had not changed dramatically in the previous 60 years, and Calvin would have seen nothing curious about the 1870s' promise of "photographs finished in India ink, crayon and watercolours." He also could not have recognized the irony of "catarrh cigarettes," a medicinal product offered to ailing students in 1878 "for the cure and relief of catarrh, asthma, cold in the head, hay fever and bronchial affections. A pleasant smoke and a most wonderful and instantaneous relief."

Queen's College Journal staff, 1891

The hoary debate about the birthplace of organized hockey may never be laid to rest. Kingston has staked its claim, as have Montreal, Ottawa and Halifax. Queen's historian Hilda Neatby ventured that "according to the recollections of Queen's graduates, the first hockey match to be played in Ontario took place in 1885 between Queen's and the Royal Military College on the lake in front of Tête de Pont Barracks." Other sources claim that the lake was not frozen that year and suggest that March 10, 1886, was the real date of the contest.

Predictably, the controversy has not interfered with the birth of a new tradition. Since 1969, Queen's and the Royal Military College have met each year on the ice of Lake Ontario during Kingston's Winterfest, garbed in 19th-century equipment, to reenact that first contest and to celebrate the history of Canada's national sport.

Senior hockey team, 1922-23

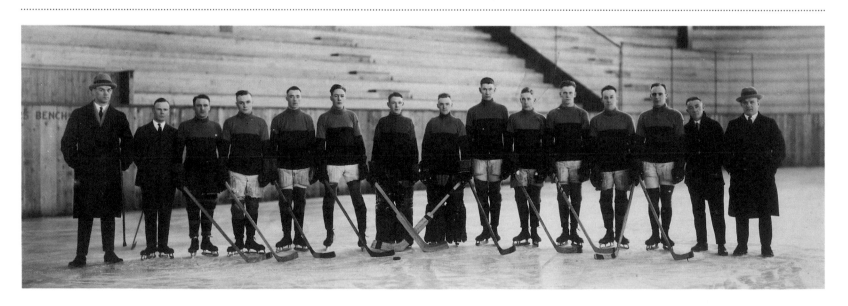

End of a successful season, 88 goals in eight games and only one loss; the hockey club of 1891-92

Class of '89, Women's Medical College

In the spring of 1880, women were allowed to attend their own classes at the Royal College of Physicians and Surgeons of Kingston — then loosely affiliated with Queen's. Until then, the study of medicine had been considered a somewhat grisly business best left to men — and tough-minded men at that. The women so completely surpassed expectations, however, that a year later, the administration decided they should simply be absorbed into the regular classes. It was a worthy beginning, and Queen's might have distinguished itself by becoming one of the first universities on the continent to offer coeducational medical training. Unfortunately, it was not to be.

After a couple of peaceful terms, tensions erupted in the 1882-83 session of a course taught by Dr. Kenneth Fenwick, one of the younger lecturers, whose dissatisfaction with various matters at the school settled on the hapless women in his class. In no time at all, he managed to make their position unbearable. Classes became an embarrassment for the women, and in the words of Elizabeth Smith (Medicine '84), life became a ''torment . . . of whispers, innuendo, derisive treading, the turning of what was never meant as unseemly into horrible meaning and the thousand and one ways that can be devised by evil minds to bring responsive smiles from their own kind.''

When the women eventually complained about the lecturer's behaviour, a flood of repressed prejudice loosed itself upon them. Male students insisted that the women's complaints represented an assault on academic freedom. They threatened to leave en masse and even approached several other colleges for admission. Trinity College immediately agreed to accept them, its administrators no doubt remembering that the first nine medical students to attend Queen's had defected from Trinity in the midst of another controversy almost 30 years before. Despite pleas from the faculty, the male students forced a crisis, and the women were withdrawn from regular classes just before Christmas of 1882. They were returned to a separate programme, and it was quietly determined that no more female candidates would be accepted.

The nationwide scandal caused by the removal of women from the Royal College of Physicians and Surgeons grew almost immediately into a movement to establish independent facilities for teaching medicine to women. In June 1883, at a meeting called by several leading Kingston citizens and attended by faculty members of the Royal College and by Principal George Monro Grant of Queen's, it was resolved that the Women's Medical College would be established by October of that same year. The financial foundations were laid with the promise of $200 per year from Dr. Jennie Trout. Four days after the meeting in Kingston, Toronto doctors who had earlier rejected a plan for a women's medical school reversed their decision, and upon hearing that the Kingston college would open on October 2, they scheduled theirs to open on October 1.

Over the next decade, the Kingston Women's Medical College graduated 42 doctors. Some returned and served as professors, and in 1889, Alice McGillivray accepted the position of Subdean of the Women's Medical College. Originally housed in City Hall, the college eventually acquired its own lodging at 75 Union Street. Caught between tightening finances and dwindling enrolment, however, the college closed in the fall of 1894. The remaining students concluded their studies at the larger schools by then firmly established in Toronto and Montreal.

Anatomy Learning Centre, Botterell Hall

Meds' orientation, 1915; medical students were the first to have their faces painted

"The Senate forbids the use of
physical violence on any person as
part of initiation activities at Queen's
University. The consent of the
victim does not make such violence
permissible or justifiable."
— Queen's Senate Minutes, 1970s

Dishevelment

The more things change, as they say, the more they stay the same. That includes the dress code for Queen's during orientation week. In the 1980s, new arrivals at the University donned an assortment of sometimes controversial outfits that ranged from kilts and purple faces to coveralls emblazoned with the student's year and, often, a crude caption stencilled on the behind.

In the 1930s, only the details varied. Women were obliged to wear one black sock and one white sock, a tricolour beret and a large placard listing their name, address and weight. They were also forbidden to wear cosmetics. First-year Arts students painted their fingernails bright red, wore soothers on strings and carried their books in a potato sack.

Engineering students were forbidden to shave and expected to toot an imaginary horn at every street corner. They were also required to drag their books behind them in baskets, which the more mechanically adept fitted with wheels.

The medical faculty — practising a curious rite that has since been taken over by Applied Science — stained their faces. Instead of gentian violet, however, they used Mercurochrome to paint a large "M" on each medical frosh's forehead.

In addition, each faculty wore neckties in flowing silk ribbon of the appropriate faculty colours, and everyone, of course, wore a tam.

Engineering "tradition"

First Women

Women first entered Queen's as full-time candidates in the fall of 1880. In this arena, Queen's most assuredly did not break new ground. Mount Allison University in Sackville, New Brunswick, had admitted women in 1858, and Oberlin College, in Oberlin, Ohio, had graduated its first women in 1841, the same year that Queen's received its Charter.

In fact, however, women had been attending classes at the College since 1869, when an English class was created for them. Classes in rhetoric and logic and natural history were added in 1870, and by 1876, Kingston women were welcomed into the College's regular chemistry and logic classes — subjects requested by a Miss de St. Remy, headmistress of a local girls' school. From the beginning, the faculty and administration took a keen interest in the progress of women students. Predictably, it was a subject of some controversy, and men like Professor John Watson were forced to keep up a battle of words against more conservative elements both inside the College and out. Yet along with the defence of principles of equality, there was very real encouragement provided and personal concern that showed in ways both large and small. In 1884, when Queen's College granted degrees to its first women graduates, Chancellor Sandford Fleming (who in his youth had worked as a cartographer and illustrator) designed and ordered a decorative pin to be awarded to the first woman Arts graduate, Eliza Fitzgerald. Principal George Monro Grant obtained a copy of the pin to be presented to the only other female Arts graduate in that inaugural year, Annie Fowler. In addition, Fitzgerald took the gold medal in classics for her year.

The presence of women in regular classes at Queen's did not, of course, eliminate strong gender prejudices. Many of the biases present when Queen's was 50 years old have survived another century. At the least, there have been some fortuitous consequences. Women, compelled to take responsibility for their own affairs, established an association of graduates during the early 20th century, and the group, the Queen's University Alumnae Association, initiated the residence movement at Queen's and planned, financed and administered the first on-campus multi-unit living accommodation: Ban Righ Hall.

The Men's Medal

For every group trying to advance to its rightful place in society, there is resistance to overcome, and the experience of women at Queen's University is no exception. But even intolerance has its absurd moments. During the early years of the century, a gold medal for proficiency in German was offered to Queen's on the condition that it be awarded to men only. Although Principal Daniel Miner Gordon pointed out that a majority of the German scholars were women — a senior class might well be made up entirely of female students — and that the medal would be of greater use if they were included, the would-be benefactor remained adamant. And there Queen's hung — caught between the tempting offer of support on the one side and all that is right and reasonable on the other. The incident was a brief, excruciating pause in the history of the University. Fortunately, another friend of Queen's came forward and resolved the administration's quandary by providing a gold medal that could be offered to all qualified students.

Women students, class of 1914

In the late 19th century, William Lawton Goodwin put rubber boots on science at Queen's and then gave it a hard hat to wear. A young man of powerful scientific intellect, Goodwin earned scholarships that took him from tiny Baie Verte, New Brunswick, to the University of Edinburgh, the University of London and on to Heidelberg, Germany, where he studied with the great chemist Robert Wilhelm Bunsen. When he arrived at Queen's in 1883, his interests shifted from the academic to the practical world, and with Professor Nathan Fellowes Dupuis and Principal George Monro Grant, Goodwin conceived of the Kingston School of Mining and Agriculture. In 1893, he became its first director.

Goodwin recognized an even wider need for education in the mining industry, and he made it his project in the school's early years to travel throughout eastern Ontario, the most active mining area in the province at the close of the 19th century, gathering miners and prospectors into local meeting halls and schoolhouses for instruction in mineralogy and geology.

As the first head of the School of Mining and Agriculture, Goodwin began with little more than a good idea and a clear sense of the importance of his task. He borrowed teachers from other departments at Queen's and also from the Royal Military College. Goodwin decided that all areas of engineering should be taught; he established a strong staff and, during his tenure, built the reputation that the faculty has enjoyed ever since.

When Goodwin retired after 36 years, he once again returned to the task of instructing prospectors. He travelled throughout Ontario for eight years and, in 1927, retired again, setting down the fruits of his long experience in the *Prospectors' Handbook*. Goodwin died in January 1941, the University's centennial year.

Magnetic separator, mining engineering lab, Goodwin Hall

A teacher, scientist and prospector, William Goodwin was also the man who designed Carruthers Hall, the first building devoted to the study of chemistry at a Canadian university. As well, he brought electric lighting to Queen's and to Kingston. Goodwin's description of the event appeared in the March 1941 edition of *The Queen's Review*:

"Electric lighting was started in the old Limestone City by a university professor. With no money to buy machinery, with nothing but an idea, it looked hopeless. But I, the professor, could not see it that way.

"At the Locomotive Works, an early type of internal-combustion gas engine was being tried out. I offered to install one in the basement of the School of Mining building if the management would make us a present of it. It was done, and so we were over the first fence.

"Then, with a letter of introduction from the invincible Principal Grant, I went to Peterborough and told the Canadian General Electric Company such a convincing story that it gave me a generator.

"The unthinking reader of this story may jump to the conclusion that my troubles were all over, that the job was done. He would be wrong. The generator was all right, an easygoing reliable machine, but we had that gas engine to reckon with. Its ignition apparatus was not complicated, just a tube heated by a gas jet; it was simple but unreliable, for reasons which I understood and tried to remedy, with moderate success only.

"There were other uncertainties about that engine. It was decidedly temperamental. When the janitor, Alfred Dean, could not make it go, Engineer Hiscock was sent up from the Locomotive Works. After a long trial, he also failed and gave it up. Then the high-brow theorist, the professor, took it in hand and made the plaguey thing go.

"So I had my lecture room wired and was soon giving evening lectures by electric lights served by that generator."

Athletes at Queen's in the late 1800s were a homeless lot who spent much of their energy regularly petitioning the Board of Trustees for a space in which to exercise. In 1880, a gymnasium was designated in the rear of the Old Medical Building, and it served well enough. It was the site of some of the College's first spectator-sports events: exhibitions put on by gymnastics classes and "specimens of wrestling." One of its drawbacks, however, was its location directly beneath the medical school's dissecting room. Unidentified, and therefore all the more horrifying, "liquids" occasionally leaked through the ceiling onto the gymnasts' heads.

"Trials of strength and skill . . . besides developing the muscular frame, would also develop a high and noble spirit of manliness."

— *Queen's College Journal*, 1874

Not the most retiring young men on campus, they were, in fact, a conspicuous bunch, involved in athletics, clubs and the student newspaper and known for their practical jokes. But during their time at Queen's, they received neither credit nor blame for their most outrageous stunt.

In the late 1890s, a new building had been added to the campus. Humble compared with the limestone edifices around it, the wooden structure was nonetheless coveted not only by the rapidly expanding science programme but also by the students' Athletics Committee, which had contributed significantly to the cost of its construction and wanted to use part of the facility as a gymnasium. When Professor Nathan Fellowes Dupuis, the Dean of Practical Science, was awarded virtually all of the space and the athletes were granted only a bit of room in the attic and a shower in the basement, a suitable response was quietly plotted.

Dupuis called his new building the Mechanical Laboratory, a somewhat glorious name for a machine shop, and thereby himself sowed the seeds of a simple revenge. With the assistance of "Duke" McGee, the icemaker at the rink, who was persuaded to leave a ladder outside at the first snowfall, a perfect crime was executed. Some paint and a brush purchased in Buffalo, New York — and therefore untraceable in small-town Kingston — and the cover of darkness were all it took. By morning, a new name was splashed across the east wall of the building: Tool House.

As amusing as the prank may have been to many, it struck Dupuis as personally disrespectful, and he threatened to resign if the guilty parties did not step forward immediately. The only incriminating evidence, however, was the paint in the moustache of the man with the brush; his coconspirators convinced him that shaving was a small price to pay for their continued status as students at Queen's. Investigations were launched, but in time, the whole matter simply faded into legend. In 1929, *The Queen's Review*, like a younger sibling telling tales out of school, faithfully recorded the names of the merry vandals. "Hambone" McLean did the painting, while Guy Curtis steadied the ladder. Their colleagues included Harry Nimmo (Arts '98; LL.D. '19), "Beeze" Williams (Arts '03; Medicine '04), G.F. Weatherhead (Arts '98; Medicine '03) and Lawrence Newlands (Science '99).

Early Queen's wrestlers practised at their peril in a basement under the dissecting room

Women's basketball, played in the attic of the Old Arts Building, was Jimmy Bews' first involvement with athletics at Queen's. Although he officially became physical director of Queen's in 1907, Bews began his career five years earlier as a volunteer instructor. His first task was fashioning baskets for the women's games "from barrel hoops, with leather thongs for nets." He also made backboards from the materials provided by male students, which he described as "a pile of boards, weather-beaten and suspiciously like the remainder of a fence that enclosed a portion of the grounds."

In those early days, the baskets were closed on the bottom, and some of the greatest excitement involved retrieving the ball after a point was scored. According to Bews, "It was only a tall and extremely active girl who could jump high enough to dislodge the ball." A broom handle was always kept at the ready, and the trickiest part of the game was poking the ball free so that play could be resumed.

As reported in the December 1, 1910, *Queen's University Journal*, "Tuesday, the 22nd [of November], was a notable day in the history of basketball at Queen's, for on that day, for the first time, the ladies' basketball team played before the public view." That notable day was followed by a notable season, with each week's games recounted in some detail by the campus paper. The *Journal*'s self-described "sporting scribe," an eager fan and effusive reporter, admitted to being hazy on the details of a game reported in the January 25, 1911, issue, explaining that he had also served as referee and could remember only the final score with any certainty. For the most part, however, games received careful scrutiny, with extravagant praise for "short, fast passing, quick running, hard checking and some really splendid shooting." Queen's women occasionally played against the YWCA, but most games were between teams formed of women from the different years.

A year later, the public games ended, without any explanation for the disappointed fans. On the front page of the new larger-format *Queen's Journal*, a tiny subhead announced on December 8, 1911, "Ladies Games Closed to Masculine Admirers." In place of the previous year's enthusiasm, there was only a concluding observation that "the sporting scribe is left out in the cold."

"Miss Grace Dunlop was nominated by Miss Kelly as Rep. on Committee to buy a new basketball to replace the one lost in Montreal."

— Levana Athletic Board of Control Minutes, October 17, 1923

Before the years of formal interuniversity competition, women's basketball at Queen's required more organizational skill than athletic prowess. Games with out-of-town rivals demanded impressive preparations. Under the auspices of the Levana Athletic Board of Control, a letter of invitation was composed and sent to McGill in Montreal or Varsity in Toronto or to a women's organization in Napanee, Gananoque, Ottawa or even across the St. Lawrence River in Potsdam, New York. If patience brought a positive reply, plans were made for taxi rides from the train station and for the provision of accommodation and food for the visitors. Since such matters involved costs, a benefit dance was often planned, preferably to coincide with the presence of the visiting team. On occasion, the Levana Athletic Board of Control would receive assistance from the University's Athletic Board of Control and would then divert any profit from the dance back into the larger group. The details of all such arrangements kept several young women busy each year, and along with the records of their correspondence with other universities — on such issues as the standardization of rules for women's basketball —the minutes of their meetings between 1922 and 1955 filled almost 300 handwritten pages.

Levana Interyear Basketball Champions, 1920

"Its proximity to large deposits of iron, gold, lead, silver, phosphates, mica and other minerals, to vast deposits of marl and clay, to good agricultural and grazing land, to extensive quarries of red sandstone and limestone, to great tracts of hard- and soft-wood timber, to lakes and rivers valuable for fish, navigation and hydraulics make it peculiarly well suited for such an institution."
— from a letter circulated by the members of the organizing committee to found the School of Mining and Agriculture in Kingston

Physics research, Stirling Hall

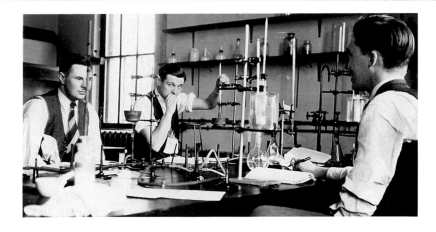

"We think that we have a good chance of progressing to even better things."

— Douglas S. Ellis, Faculty of Applied Science, *The Queen's Review*, 1953

The history of the Faculty of Applied Science begins with some baffling sleight of hand that transformed one school into two and eventually allowed them to become one again. In 1893, the Kingston School of Mining and Agriculture officially commenced operations "as a corporation under the act respecting benevolent and other societies," with capital stock of $100,000. Officially independent of Queen's, which was for purposes of funding a denominational Presbyterian College, the school remained entirely eligible for provincial government support. That same year, the Queen's Faculty of Practical Science appeared and offered courses in chemistry and mineralogy, mechanical engineering, civil engineering, electrical engineering, mining engineering and biology leading to medicine. Professor Nathan Fellowes Dupuis became Dean of Practical Science, Professor William Lawton Goodwin director of the School of Mining and Agriculture.

Although the departments later merged to form the Faculty of Applied Science, there was no official connection between the two — the one eligible for government funds and the other ineligible because of its status within a denominational College. Nonetheless, the students enrolled in the two schools shared a building — originally a frame structure tacked onto the north side of Carruthers Hall. They also shared professors; indeed, they shared classrooms. The distinction between the two schools was little more than a subterfuge designed by Principal George Monro Grant and condoned by Ontario Premier Oliver Mowat to circumvent the legal technicality that would otherwise have prevented the provincial government from providing additional funds to Queen's.

Of course, not everyone was quite as tolerant of the Principal's ploy. Remarked University of Toronto Professor John C. MacLennan, who still harboured resentment years later: "Grant had this Province on its knees."

After a quiet summer, campus neighbourhoods return to life

Slumming

The student "ghetto" has evolved over time. Reacting to changes in the City of Kingston, it has drawn back from areas of rising property value and reached out toward rental units wherever they are. The ghetto has also retreated before the expansion of campus, but the heart of student housing always lies alongside the University, sometimes in the very shadow of its buildings. For thousands of alumni, Queen's means classrooms and laboratories, but it also means Collingwood, Albert and Frontenac streets. It means walking along Barrie Street or University Avenue, and it means a home somewhere near the corner of Clergy and Earl streets.

Balconies with sun, a key rental feature

Daniel Miner Gordon (1902-16): A New Century

Cut from the same cloth as the late George Monro Grant, Daniel Miner Gordon was a clergyman, born in Pictou, Nova Scotia, and educated at the Pictou Academy and at Glasgow University. Like Grant, he enjoyed a reputation for diplomacy within the Church, and he, too, had assisted Sandford Fleming in his early explorations and survey work in the West. He enjoyed travel and possessed the same vigorous capacity for work as did his predecessor. In short, Gordon stood for the same values as had George Monro Grant.

Gordon's 1902 appointment as Principal came in the midst of the distress and confusion swirling in the vacuum left by Grant's death. One campus faction thought that the Trustees should promote the immensely popular professor of philosophy John Watson, then Vice-Principal, to the job of Principal.

When Watson refused the nomination, a bitter controversy led to the choice of James Barclay. After he, too, declined, Gordon, a professor at the Presbyterian College in Halifax, became the obvious candidate.

As his tenure progressed, Gordon proved the wisdom of his appointment. He combined the sagacity needed to live in the long and potent shadow of his predecessor with the determination necessary to carry the University through tremendous changes. He oversaw the separation of Queen's from the Presbyterian Church — a financial decision that nonetheless required years of fierce and often very emotional debate at Church assemblies — and he held Queen's together when World War I threatened in so many ways to pull it apart, draining away not just students and funds but also the youthful idealism of a generation.

Principal Daniel Miner Gordon

Communion in the historic second-floor Morgan Memorial Chapel, Theological Hall

The separation of Queen's from the Presbyterian Church required more than a decade of cajoling, recrimination and debate. The ongoing debate married questions of the highest religious and educational ideals with the crassest of concerns about financial sponsorship and individual security. For all its significance, it did not rank among the University's finest moments.

Principal George Monro Grant had watched as his successful attempts to expand the institution outstripped the funds available from donors; because the College was considered a denominational body, however, it did not qualify for government support. Caught in this trap, Grant set out to disentangle the affairs of Church and College for good, and by the time of his death in 1902, he had succeeded in amassing the support he needed.

Yet the power Grant had wielded revealed itself even more clearly with his passing. Without his dynamic influence, the consensu he had nurtured devolved into 10 years' worth of discontent, and the already contentious question of religious influence and financial support fairly boiled when the matter of pensions for professors entered the discussion.

American industrialist Andrew Carnegie, reasoning that professors pursue a worthy life's work without opportunity to acquire wealth to secure their retirement, had endowed a vast fund to provide pensions for academics. But because the foundation believed that the Church should provide for its own, denominational colleges did not have access to the fund. Technicalities left Queen's scholars out in the cold, eligible for neither Church support nor philanthropic assistance. As a consequence, some of the College's foremost teachers became vigorous proponents of separation. Many in the Church accused them of simple avarice.

In the end, the opponents of separation conceded that a theological college affiliated with an independent university would ensure a good Christian influence upon the students. Thus, in 1912, Queen's University, complete with a new constitution, stepped free of the gentle ties that bound it to the Presbyterian Church and moved forward into a secular future.

During the course of the protracted discussions, Carnegie himself had precipitously, and mistakenly, assured his friend James Douglas that Queen's had been added to the list of institutions eligible for funds. On the basis of this information, three Queen's professors were persuaded to retire. When the error was brought to light, Principal Daniel Miner Gordon made a special appeal to Carnegie, who agreed to pay those men's pensions personally.

Theological Hall, built 1880

Queen's owes its library to James Douglas's father, to his spirit of adventure and to his gullible investment in a worthless Quebec copper mine. Trained as a physician and surgeon, the elder Douglas had no business speculating in mine development. In time, however, that same spirit sparked one of the most extravagantly successful careers in the history of North American mining. And from that great fortune came the money to build Queen's stately central library.

James Douglas, already trained as a Presbyterian minister, received a bachelor's degree from Queen's in 1858. In the summer of 1868, Douglas, determined to redeem his father's investment, pursued a series of successful investigations that led to a new method for the treatment of mixed copper, silver and gold ores. The process attracted notice in the United States, and in 1875, Douglas moved to Pennsylvania to supervise improvements to the Chemical Copper Company's extraction plant there. Five years later, he did preliminary assessments of deposits at Bisbee, Arizona, for a New York company and recommended acquiring claims adjacent to the Copper Queen Mine. From that point on, his professional reputation gathered an impressive momentum. Eventually, he was named the president of the Copper Queen Consolidated Mining Company. He became a very wealthy man and, according to *The New York Times*, "one of the foremost metal and mining authorities in the world."

Douglas became as adept at giving away money as at making it. Both McGill and Queen's benefited from his philanthropic generosity. In 1910, he endowed the Douglas Chair in Canadian and Colonial History at Queen's, the first position of its kind in the country. With his usual flair — he once donated $375,000 to Memorial Hospital in New York City in the form of 3 ¾ grams of radium — he accompanied the history endowment with an actual ceremonial chair, a veritable throne carved in Burmese teak.

In the years that followed, his munificence grew with the University's needs. He accepted the position of Chancellor in 1915 — filling the void left by Sir Sandford Fleming's death — and as Queen's buckled under the financial pressures of wartime, Chancellor Douglas personally stepped forward with the resources needed to keep the University afloat. He signed over more than $100,000 for operating costs alone during the war years. Another $150,000 formed the basis of the library building fund, and a further $100,000 contributed to the reconstruction of Kingston General Hospital. Over the years, his donations totalled nearly $1 million, an unbounded fortune during the first decades of the century.

Throughout his life, Douglas also published articles on topics that ranged from metallurgy and rail transport to "The Status of Women in New England and New France." While a man of God by training and an ascendant businessman, Douglas saw the world through the eyes of a scholar. A library is a fitting memorial.

Four million references, plus

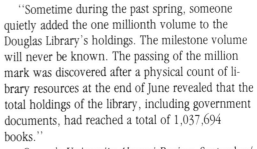

"Sometime during the past spring, someone quietly added the one millionth volume to the Douglas Library's holdings. The milestone volume will never be known. The passing of the million mark was discovered after a physical count of library resources at the end of June revealed that the total holdings of the library, including government documents, had reached a total of 1,037,694 books."
— *Queen's University Alumni Review*, September/ October 1973

Bicycles, fall 1989

Sir Sandford Fleming

Queen's elected Sandford Fleming as its second Chancellor in 1880 and reelected him three years later and again three years after that and then again and again and again. Like the regular ticking of a 35-year clock, each successive term of office reaffirmed Queen's attachment to this extraordinary man. Only his death in 1915 brought to an end a mutually affectionate and satisfying relationship.

The story of Fleming's life is usually an account of his great accomplishments. It leaves the distinct impression that it is history's fortune that Fleming was born to the 19th century and sent early to the British North American colonies, because only an untouched continent could have absorbed his utterly boundless energies, and nothing but surveying the wilderness and stitching the Imperial British world together with railroads and transoceanic telegraph cables could have satisfied his ambition. But Fleming's life also included a great friendship, a quieter, firmer measure of his life's achievements, a collaboration that eventually focused its combined energies on Queen's and benefited the institution in ways beyond measure.

When Fleming took up his position as Chancellor, he and George Monro Grant resumed a partnership that had already endured the tests of time and hard travel, near death by starvation, weariness and bitter cold. They rejoined a friendship that had taken them across the continent in 1872, plotting the route of the Canadian Pacific Railway, a trip that took them into the breathtaking beauty of the almost unknown world in the West and the North. Five years before his appointment to the Principal's job at Queen's, Grant had accompanied Fleming as secretary on the original survey expedition. The two men who would help determine the shape and future of Canadian university education already ranked among the country's great explorers.

Spurred on by Fleming's example and encouragement, Grant possessed the vision — and confidence — to transform Queen's into a university with ambitious plans for the approaching century.

''Let me advise you not to throw away or neglect your grand opportunities,'' Fleming told Queen's students in his inaugural address as Chancellor. ''Do not trifle with your precious college days. You may not all win prizes or attract attention at examinations. The race is not always to the swift. Do not be discouraged if your morning star does not shine brightly. The shining may come later on in the day. Bring to bear on your work earnestness of purpose, self-reliance, perseverance, sobriety of speech and of behaviour, and you will be certain to vanquish every difficulty. Be determined to spend your college days to some purpose, and you will surely carry with you into the world treasures which no thief can steal and a fortune which no adversity can take from you.''

Sir Sandford Fleming, Chancellor, 1880-1915

A talented football and baseball player and a star of the eastern Ontario lacrosse circuit until he was 40, Alfie Pierce was the son of an American slave who had escaped to Canada. Pierce dedicated himself, his time, his energies and his boundless affections to the generations of impudent young men who played out the most glorious moments of their youth on Queen's football fields.

From the age of 15, when football captain Guy Curtis — with all the thoughtless bigotry of the age — named the orphaned teenager "team mascot," until his final years as a legendary repository of football tradition, Pierce was a constant presence at Queen's. He served originally as trainer, or "rubber," as he was known in the early days; and the players themselves paid his way to out-of-town games. He also did duty as an assistant coach with both the hockey team and the football squad, and he helped with the boxers, often standing in as a formidable sparring partner.

Although there was no formal title for his position at the University, Alfie Pierce embodied the heart of Queen's football tradition. He cheered his first team on only seven years after R.A. Gordon and the brothers C. Jackson and J. Fred Booth brought the game to the campus in 1882. As if each generation of players had graduated and somehow bequeathed its most valuable moments to his care, Pierce became a symbol of gridiron heroics. He remembered. As the names changed and the rules of the game evolved and as more elaborate equipment was added to the original outfit of jerseys, pants and boots with leather strips tacked onto the soles for traction, Pierce recalled it all: the great teams and the bad teams, the losses, the rainy days and the tumultuous moments of glory.

For years, Pierce lived in the Jock Harty Arena during the winter and under the Richardson Stadium grandstand in the summer months. Even after his semiretirement, he remained a fixture, somehow surviving on a meagre pension from the Athletic Board of Control. Few football alumni ever returned to the campus without stopping by to see their sage trainer and friend. In his deep, throaty voice — legend has it that he damaged his vocal cords cheering for his boys — Pierce always made them welcome. He held the young athletes of Queen's in high esteem, but the history of the University has its own priority: more alumni of the era before Pierce's death in 1951 remember the great fan of Queen's football than remember any one of those players for whom he cheered.

Alfie's, named for a campus legend

Alfie Pierce, far right, trainer with the senior rugby team, 1900

Boardinghouse Blues

Before the era of University-administered residences, the main source of student accommodation was private boardinghouses, which existed largely to serve the seasonal University population. Although prices changed over the years, the standard arrangement remained the same: there was one fee for the room and another fee for board, or food. According to some, the wise student ate in one establishment and slept in another. If one situation fell through, the argument went, at least half of life's necessities would still be attended to.

The quality of the accommodations varied, of course, and as with good student rental apartments today, coveted positions passed from friend to friend as generations of students came and went.

"The custom in vogue at Queen's with regard to board and lodging is intolerable. It is a sordid business, this annual search, from house to house, for decent lodging and board and all the petty vexations which the relationship of lodger and landlady implies. The unsanitary and disagreeable surroundings which prevail in the typical boardinghouse are but poor incentives to study. The ill health of many students can be traced to the 'boardinghouse.' "
— *Queen's University Journal*, October 20, 1910

Rules to Live By

"From the front hall up, the house was really divided in two. On each side, 9 to 11 girls lived on the two upper floors, and each side had one bathroom. Baths were arranged on a definite schedule, and in order to work us all in, some had to be taken in spares between classes. The trading of times that went on was prodigious, especially on the nights of dances."
— Lorraine Shortt, Arts '20

"No member of the House Committee shall go to restaurants after 10:00 p.m."
— from the Avonmore house rules

The Hencoop

For two years following the turn of the century, a women's residence operated on William Street. An uncertain effort begun by a few women graduates and professors' wives, it was superseded almost immediately by Maplehurst, a mid-19th-century building on the corner of Earl and Clergy streets that served as a women's residence for 23 years. While the William Street effort never amounted to anything more than a chaperoned rental house with a weekly budget of $4, it nevertheless launched the entire programme of University-sponsored accommodation at Queen's.

Limited space at Maplehurst — also known as The Hencoop, an originally derisive label that the women wisely co-opted and made their own — brought demands in 1916 for a second facility. The Avonmore, also on William Street, opened the following year, even as plans and fund raising were under way for an official residence on campus.

Until the opening of Ban Righ Hall in 1925, the two semiofficial residences were home to the luckiest of the young women who came to Kingston to study at Queen's. To many who roomed elsewhere (they were called "grubbers" or "mealers"), Maplehurst and Avonmore provided food each day and a place for conversation and friendship.

Residents of The Hencoop, 1917-18

The future Dean Elspeth Baugh learned that she was moving to Kingston and to Queen's in 1936 when her friend, the storekeeper, showed her a copy of *The Edmonton Journal* with her father's photograph on the front page. She promptly burst into tears. She was 7 years old, and her father was Robert C. Wallace, the newly appointed Principal of Queen's University.

Elspeth Wallace grew up at Queen's, in Summerhill, the Principal's residence. She and her family summered on nearby Garden Island, and as a young woman, she had the uncommon experience of attending a university run by her father. (Greeted by dozens of students every day, Principal Wallace did not always recognize his own daughter when they passed each other on campus. He was unfailingly polite, however, and always tipped his hat courteously.) She went on to do an M.A. in clinical psychology at the University of Michigan in 1949.

In 1950, Elspeth Wallace moved back to Kingston and began to work as a psychologist. In the same year, she also married Dr. Charles Baugh, and between 1953 and 1967, she raised six children. After resuming her career as a psychologist, Elspeth Baugh enrolled at York University in 1972 and received a Marty Memorial Scholarship from the Queen's University Alumnae Association; she graduated with a Ph.D. in 1978.

When Baugh returned to Queen's in 1980, she did far more than simply return to her childhood home. In taking on the responsibilities of the Dean of Women, she accepted a position that many considered to be an anachronism. Because the job had grown out of the particular needs of the small number of women on campus, it seemed out of step with the fully coeducational campus of 55 years later. During the first 10 years of her tenure, however, increasing social pressures, the demands of women students and Dean Baugh's own convictions redefined the office. A 1989 Principal's Advisory Committee that met to consider abolishing the position instead reaffirmed the Dean's crucial new role, both for the students and for the administration, as a monitor of gender issues during changing times at the University.

Elspeth Wallace, Principal's daughter

Neighbourhood children and Queen's students share a longstanding winter tradition

"Let us throw aside this idea of keeping women in the background. It is one of the last relics of barbarism."

— *Queen's College Journal*, 1881

Building Budgets During Cautious Times

On October 11, 1919, Queen's graduate Marion Redden rose before the first postwar meeting of the Queen's University Alumnae Association (QUAA) and announced that the prewar residence building fund of $16,500 had, through careful management, grown to more than $40,000. The QUAA's original goal of $50,000 was now within reach.

Many present at that meeting would have blanched had they foreseen what the next six years held: the months of struggle in which the idea of a building proved to be infinitely simpler than the reality of constructing one. Along with constant fund-raising campaigns came endless rounds of architectural consultations and engineering problems to be resolved. As well as the war against steadily rising costs, there were unexpected battles with the University's own Trustees, whose lack of faith created additional obstacles.

In fact, construction estimates had leaped from $50,000 to $160,000, and the alumnae convinced the University to match half the required cost, up to the sum of $80,000. In return, the Trustees demanded ownership of the building. The alumnae acquiesced but insisted on retaining "a large share in the control of the management" of the residence. When the Trustees further required that the QUAA underwrite the expected annual deficit for the residence's operations, the group again calmly agreed, this time on the condition that any surplus be dedicated "entirely to women's residence purposes." (According to Charlotte Whitton's record of the events, by 1939, "this surplus was to exceed $100,000 and become the basis of a QUAA request to add a new wing.") Although it nearly caused a breach with the University, the alumnae secured personal bonds when the Trustees refused to allow work to begin because last-minute costs had again taken the project over budget. Unwilling to trust the women's already demonstrated money-raising abilities, the ever cautious Board of Trustees required legal guarantees that even the final $15,000 be accounted for before the walls went up.

Relaxing in the common room, Ban Righ Hall

The Hall of the Wife of the King

In the 1920s, the Queen's University Alumnae Association had rejected the name "Banrighinn" — from the Queen's yell — as the name for its new residence. The well-known owner of the local Kingston theatre was named Dinny Brannigan, and the Queen's women wanted no possibility of such an undignified confusion. It was Professor Malcolm Macgillivray, the Gaelic authority at the University, who suggested the name Ban Righ Hall — "the Hall of the Wife of the King," that is, Queen's Hall. And so the new residence was named.

Morning rush hour

Ban Righ Hall at Last

As Ban Righ Hall was being planned and built, there were never more than just over 300 active members of the Queen's University Alumnae Association (QUAA). Yet those few were very active indeed. They gave not only their money but also their time and ingenuity. They held dances and dinner parties in which the alumnae charged for the food and even sold the flowers from their own gardens to the captive guests. Ada Birch, the association secretary, sold newspapers and magazines for two years, contributing the profits to the fund. Ottawa alumnae sponsored actress Julia Arthur in *Saint Joan*, one of the last events staged in the historic Russell Theatre; one performance brought in nearly $1,300. The women made sure that the University paid interest on the alumnae money held back by the Board of Trustees prior to actual construction. And before approval for construction had been given, the alumnae saved nearly $3,000 on materials by arranging with Kingston stonecutters to quarry during the winter at 15 cents per hour less than their usual rates. The stone was stored on the site and stood as a reminder to anyone who doubted for a moment that the project would succeed.

From architectural design and general contracting to interior decoration, the industry and expertise of the QUAA transformed an idea into a women's residence. Since 1925, Ban Righ Hall has been home to thousands of Queen's women.

The Baby Unit Goes to War

At the turn of the century, military matters at Queen's were as much a source of humour as anything else. The Boer War proved merely diverting. The December 21, 1899, *Queen's University Journal* joked about an imaginary "Science Hall Light Infantry" doing battle at "Nathansdorp," an equally imaginary South African battlefield, most likely named in honour of Queen's own peaceable man of science, Nathan Fellowes Dupuis. Even a decade later, as angry prophets around the world began to speak of an impending clash of European powers, the *Journal* still poked fun at zealous "drills at the Armouries of the Fifth Field Company, Canadian Engineers, our baby military unit." With the declaration of war in August 1914, however, the ironic tone fell away like a smile chased from a face.

Two days after Britain's (and thus Canada's) entry into the conflict, the Militia Department at Ottawa telegraphed Major Alexander Macphail, the commanding officer of the "baby unit," and ordered the Queen's engineers to Valcartier, Quebec. Three weeks later, students scarcely returned from their summer jobs across the country left Kingston once more and, upon their arrival at Valcartier, were immediately assigned the task of laying out a camp to accommodate the thousands of young soldiers being assembled there. The atmosphere changed abruptly, and humour was replaced with a perhaps naïve but deadly serious enthusiasm.

Many of the troops assigned to Valcartier continued on overseas. The remainder eventually returned to Kingston where they spearheaded a recruitment drive that resulted in a new Field Company organized under Professor Lindsay Malcolm. That second group — mainly students and graduates — went overseas in January 1915.

Parading on the Lower Campus; Queen's Canadian Officers' Training Corps, January 1916

"At the end of 1915, 4 of 10 male undergraduates at Queen's were in uniform."

— Kathryn M. Bindon, *Queen's Men, Canada's Men*

At Queen's, as elsewhere in the British Empire, the thundering guns of Europe posed an undeniable threat to the orderliness of the world. As an institution conceived and built in the quiet shadow of the Pax Britannica and dedicated to communicating the ideals of King and Empire, the University community undoubtedly felt even more closely threatened than most, and its reaction was strong; beneath the excitement grew a powerful sense of purpose.

At the centre of the Queen's war effort stood Principal Daniel Miner Gordon. Even prior to the outbreak of hostilities, he had been a strong advocate of universal military training for young men, and he encouraged militia activities on campus, lending essential support to the Canadian Officers' Training Corps. He travelled to the Valcartier, Quebec, training grounds, where Queen's first volunteers spent the early weeks of the war, and in the years of fighting that followed, he sent Christmas cards to each of the students overseas. Personal condolences from the Principal were written to the parents of every Queen's man killed in combat.

Under Gordon's administration, the University offered every possible encouragement to those who wished to enlist. Academic credit was given to students who interrupted their year and signed up in the spring of 1915, provisions were made for examinations to be written while abroad, and medical students who signed on with Dr. Frederick Etherington's hospital attended lectures by their enlisted professors. During a period of critical underfunding, the University continued to pay enlisted faculty half of their full-time salaries.

There were those who resisted the wave of patriotic fever that swept the University. The *Queen's Journal*, although it assiduously reported the daily details of the war and once declaimed in boldface type that "every student should be in training or be able to give a reason for not being so," also defended those who did not enlist by pointing out that Queen's was an institution dedicated to teaching people to think for themselves. Those whose consciences instructed them to stay home were to be respected every bit as much as those whose consciences told them to go.

The quiet dignity of the campus belied its constant need for funds

Bruce Taylor (1917-30): Million-Dollar Day

Ten days after he became Principal of Queen's in 1917, Reverend R. Bruce Taylor learned that it was his immediate task to raise $500,000. Chancellor James Douglas had agreed to match that sum, but his health was failing, and there was no guarantee that the generous offer would survive his passing. Thus, in the spring of 1918, Principal and Mrs. Taylor and Queen's Registrar G.Y. Chown and his wife undertook an exhausting cross-Canada railroad journey to meet with alumni and win their financial support. Their heroic efforts, which involved travel by night and endless meetings by day, netted just under $250,000, half the required amount.

With nearly a quarter of a million dollars assured and with the air of a man who, in any case, had nothing to lose, Taylor travelled to New York and visited the philanthropic Carnegie Corporation. An earlier request from Queen's that Carnegie kick off the campaign with $100,000 had drawn a flat rejection, but this time, the fund raiser's outstretched cap already contained a considerable sum. The Carnegie Corporation agreed to double the amount already raised, and with the cooperation of the estate of Chancellor Douglas, the total automatically doubled again to $1 million. "I walked back to the hotel down Fifth Avenue," Taylor remembered, "saying to myself that life had its high spots."

Principal R. Bruce Taylor

Death of a Campus Hero

"During the war of 1914-18, a patrol of No. 2 Company, 2nd Canadian Infantry Battalion, set out from their front-line position near Dranoutre, France, to raid positions held by the German enemy. After hours spent in the dark, damp, penetrating cold of that night — February 9-10, 1916 — the patrol became heavily engaged by the enemy. Two men were wounded slightly, but the officer leading the operation, Captain George T. Richardson, fell, mortally wounded, and died at 8 o'clock on the morning of February 10 at R.E. Farm. Captain Richardson was buried at the Bailleul on Friday, February 11. The large number of soldiers of all ranks, including five general-officers, who attended the solemn burial service on the battlefield of a gallant officer, was expressive of the widespread sorrow felt for this truly brave and inspiring man.

"Captain Richardson was a native of Kingston, a senior member of the great Canadian merchant firm of James Richardson & Sons Ltd. A graduate of Queen's University and an outstanding athlete, the Captain had attained prominence as a star of the football field and the hockey arena. His name today still stands at the head of the list of those football greats who have, down through all the years, scored touchdowns for Queen's.

"George Richardson was an officer of the 14th Regiment P.W.O.R. [Princess of Wales Own Regiment] of Kingston when the war started. Without hesitation and in spite of his extensive business commitments, he joined the Kingston contingent which left for overseas service within a few days after the outbreak of the war. During the long period of hard training at Valcartier and Salisbury Plains, Captain Richardson became much loved and admired by his men. He kept himself always in first-class physical condition, and he saw to it that his command were all in A-1 condition and that their training was full and complete in every detail. His thought for the comfort and happiness of his men was an outstanding characteristic. From his own pocket, he purchased 250 pairs of extra fine boots, enough for every man in the company. From him came weekly issues of cigarettes, tobacco and other comforts for his company. Men going on leave to England after months spent at the front were given 'a little extra to spend' by the Captain. . . . He supplied his company with effective gas masks within a few days after the Germans had released the first gas cloud against the 3rd Canadian Brigade. His action was typical of the man. Realizing the danger of gas attacks, he moved quickly to provide the best possible protection for his company. Many, many were the instances of his kindly thought and financial outlay, easing the hard life of his front-line infantrymen. But he was withal a strict disciplinarian; his slogan was: 'There's a job to be done, and there's a right way to do it.' By his leadership and courage, he inspired his command so that at the time of his death, his unit was outstanding as a fighting unit. This fact was recognized by the French government, which awarded Captain Richardson the 'Legion of Honour.'

"This then sets down, all too briefly, the memories of one who served with Captain Richardson during all his service in the war, memories that 35 years of passing time have not dimmed.

"In 1921, Mr. James Richardson caused to be erected at Queen's the George Richardson Memorial Stadium, and on October 8, 1921, Mr. Richardson formally turned over the stadium to the Athletic Board as a permanent memorial to his brother.

"The bronze tablet erected on the wall of the grandstand bears the following inscription: 'Desiring to put on record in this stadium, erected by his brother in his memory, the great love and honour in which they held him, the former comrades of Captain George T. Richardson, in the field of sport and in the field of war, have set up this tablet as a memorial to his love of truth, his chivalrous honour and the high courage and devotion which filled his life and led him to his death, with the hope that in all who here contend in manly exercises, his spirit may endure.' "

— by Charles Hicks, then Secretary, Athletic Board of Control

A Commemorative Field

A community of nuns owned the property between lower Alfred and lower Albert streets, and Principal Daniel Miner Gordon, through his friendship with Archbishop Gauthier, succeeded in having it sold to Queen's. This open area — later the parking area between Mackintosh-Corry Hall and Frank Tindall Field — was the original home of Richardson Stadium.

The stadium was moved to West Campus in 1971. In a ceremony prior to the first game, a piece of sod was transplanted from the old field to the new.

Standing room only; dedication of the George Taylor Richardson Memorial Stadium, October 1921

In 1914, millionaire Major R.W. Leonard proposed to build a paramilitary barracks for use by young men attending Queen's University. Any male student could live in the buildings erected and furnished by Leonard as long as he joined the Canadian Officers' Training Corps, agreed to accept military discipline and attended military drill and lectures six hours a week. The buildings — to be located on waterfront land purchased by Leonard — would be supervised by a military officer. Disagreement over the composition of the supervisory board for this venture, however, led to the University's rejection of the offer.

Following the war, Leonard donated the land, now Leonard Field, to the University in recognition of the sacrifices to the war effort that had been made by the Queen's community. He later bequeathed $100,000 to the Queen's endowment and made further provisions for scholarships.

W.E. McNeill, after residence opening, 1955

The Vindication of W.E. McNeill

In 1919, after teaching English literature and public speaking at Queen's for 10 years, William Everett McNeill had a not unreasonable expectation that he would succeed to the head of the English department upon the retirement of James Cappon. He had, in fact, served for a time as acting department head. Instead, he became the central figure in a controversy that saw him not only passed over as department head but also demoted to the nonacademic position of University Registrar and Treasurer. "For 10 years," he later avowed bitterly, "I could hardly enter the Arts building without tears."

Despite his humiliation, McNeill proved remarkably able in his role as Registrar and Treasurer, and his wounded pride must have been somewhat soothed by the unsuccessful search for a suitable department head after he had been passed over. In six years, as many heads and acting heads were hired. McNeill, in the meantime, became an invaluable administrator, eventually accepting the Vice-Principal's job in 1930.

McNeill's vindication was utter and complete. In the disastrous years of the Depression, he was credited with saving the University from economic ruin. He cut back on all expenses except salaries and constantly guarded against any inroads upon the University's precious endowment fund. (In 1955, the first men's residence at Queen's, constructed and furnished at a cost of $1,000,000, honoured W.E. McNeill who, according to Principal W.A. Mackintosh's report to the Trustees, "had always visualized men's residences as an important part of a well-rounded university.")

Principal William Hamilton Fyfe himself claimed that McNeill did all of the work of running the University and left the Principal only the "ornamental functions." Indeed, Fyfe strenuously championed McNeill's appointment as his successor. Although McNeill himself rejected the idea, he was so respected in the University community that Chancellor James Richardson sought McNeill's personal approval before proceeding with the interview which eventually brought Principal Robert C. Wallace to Queen's.

McNeill House, the first men's residence

Stained glass adds a mediaeval air to Douglas Library's Reading Room

The Richardson Family: A Queen's Dynasty

Many great families have aided the progress of Queen's, linking themselves, generation after generation, to the affairs of the University and contributing skills, imagination, time and money. Among the "clans of Queen's," none has played a greater role than the Richardson's. In addition to its support, the family holds the unique distinction of having provided 2 of the 10 Chancellors who have served the University since the position was created in 1877 — James A. Richardson and his daughter, Agnes Benidickson, who is the current Chancellor of Queen's University.

James A. Richardson (B.A. '06), president of James Richardson & Sons Limited, grain merchants, was a financier and pioneer in the development of Canadian aviation and served Queen's as a Trustee before he became Chancellor in 1929. For 10 years, until his death in 1939, he worked to reestablish the office as an active force in the administration of the University and made his influence felt in such cru-

cial matters as the selections of Principals William Hamilton Fyfe and Robert C. Wallace.

Agnes Benidickson (B.A. '41; LL.D. '79) also became a director of James Richardson & Sons Limited, the National Trust Company Limited and the Mutual Life Assurance Company of Canada. On the occasion of her receiving a Distinguished Service Award from Queen's in 1978, the *Queen's Alumni Review* noted that "her campus visits are in the nature of homecomings. She attends meetings in a hall named for her Chancellor-father, sitting in chairs once occupied by her mother and brother as Trustees; she visits a fine community art gallery given to Queen's by her aunt and sustained to no small degree by her own good taste and practical support; she can cheer the Gaels in a stadium commemorating her uncle and know that campus libraries and lectureships are enriched by family benefactions." In 1989, Benidickson accepted reappointment to a fourth three-year term as Chancellor of Queen's University.

Study carrells, Douglas Library; seating for 950

He weighed only 176 pounds and stood under six feet tall, but in 1898, when Frederick "Teddy" Etherington entered Queen's College, his was considered a formidable stature. Before he graduated, Etherington had starred for four years on the football team and become team captain. According to the *Queen's University Journal*, "His ability as a player, his coolheadedness, sound judgment and reticence on all doubtful issues most aptly fit him to succeed to the captaincy of the Queen's armies." In Alfie Pierce's opinion, Etherington was quite simply the greatest player ever to represent Queen's. Skilled at lacrosse, he was equally impressive on the baseball diamond. As an undergraduate, he was vice-president of the Alma Mater Society when it coordinated the students' collection of funds to build Grant Hall, and he crowned his academic career by serving as valedictorian for the Class of '02.

After convocation, Etherington took up duties as a house surgeon at Kingston General Hospital. Chroniclers of Queen's history like to point out that Etherington's reputation for fairness was so great that following his graduation, he was named referee for Queen's home games. Previously, an outside official had been brought to town for such contests.

Etherington's career as an educator at Queen's began almost before he finished his own studies. In 1904, Etherington was sent to the anatomy department of Edinburgh University to observe the method of the famous British schools. By 1907, he had already served for two years as a lecturer at Queen's and been appointed a professor of anatomy. Even World War I could not interrupt his association with his alma mater, and in 1915, as hostilities spread, he organized the Number 5 Stationary Hospital, which was sent almost immediately to Europe. In 1929, he agreed to a five-year term as the Dean of the Faculty of Medicine; in 1934, he was reappointed. Succeeding the venerable Dr. J.C. Connell might well have intimidated a lesser person, but not only did Etherington maintain the high standards of his predecessor, he also oversaw a steady improvement of the faculty. In October 1943, Etherington retired to his home on University Avenue, a step away from the campus, with a full view of the University he had helped to build.

"Teddy" Etherington, circa 1900

In May 1915, they marched out Montreal Street to the Kingston junction, and then the Queen's Number 5 Stationary Hospital, headed by Dr. Frederick Etherington, departed for Montreal and from there travelled to Plymouth Harbour, England, on the Canadian Pacific Railway liner *S.S. Metagama*. Eight medical officers, one dental officer, one quartermaster and 89 other ranks all volunteered. They were staff, students and graduates, and they were accompanied by 35 nursing sisters from eastern Ontario. Three weeks later, British military authorities deposited them on St. Martin's Plain, England, where they were put in charge of a tent hospital set aside for the treatment of venereal diseases.

The Queen's medical contingent came into being only after petitions were sent to Sam Hughes, the Canadian Minister of Militia, and after direct pressure was applied by Principal Daniel Miner Gordon's son-in-law, W.F. Nickle, the Kingston-area Member of Parliament. The Imperial authorities, it seemed, had no use for medical services provided by the Dominions, and only the worsening conditions on European battlefields and Etherington's personal interviews in Ottawa finally managed to earn London's approval. Exactly 40 days after orders arrived, the assembled staff departed from Kingston.

In less than two months, the Queen's hospital in England doubled in size and began receiving wounded from the front. And by the time the staff received its official assignment and set out for Egypt, the hospital had grown again, to over 600 beds. They sailed in August, travelling the length of the Mediterranean, touching at Alexandria, Egypt, and finally landing at Cairo. Establishing themselves at the Abbassia cavalry barracks on the edge of the desert, at the apex of the Nile delta in Lower Egypt, they treated wounded soldiers from Australia and New Zealand who arrived from the tragic battle at Gallipoli. The hospital eventually expanded to more than 1,000 beds, with wards named after Queen's Principal Daniel Miner Gordon and James Douglas, the new Chancellor. During its time in the Middle East, it was upgraded to Number 7 Canadian General Hospital. In these desert facilities, the students continued their education, attending compulsory lectures twice a day.

Queen's reinforcements for Number 5 Stationary Hospital, 1915

The Campus at War

The people of Queen's responded unstintingly to the demands of war, and the campus itself was pressed into service. In December 1916, Queen's authorities learned that as many as 10,000 Canadians were to be sent home from Europe as invalids. They offered Grant Hall and the adjacent Arts building for use as a military hospital. The results were described in the June 1917 *Alumnae News*:

"What a strange place it is in these advanced days of the war, our 'good old Queen's'! What a dearth of men about the halls and grounds! Many are the evidences of war; men in khaki billeted in several of the science buildings; ammunition wagons on the old clay tennis courts; a busy Red Cross hive of workers at all hours of the day in the Old Medical Building. Strangest of all — Grant Hall, the centre of so many happy memories of undergraduate days, and the Arts building, of equally happy if less frivolous memory, have been transformed almost beyond recognition. Those stately pillars are now sheathed in white beaver-board, as are also the walls. The galleries are levelled and the floors continued partway over the centre of the hall and edged with a parapet. . . . All the stained glass in the windows has been replaced by ordinary glass. A labyrinth of bathrooms and linen cupboards fills the corridor outside the hall and barricades the main entrance. A strange transformation."

The windows of the John Deutsch University Centre's Memorial Room

Loss of the Students' Memorial Union, 1947

A sad tally was taken following World War I by Professor Herbert Wallace of the Theological College. His totals showed that 1,489 students and graduates had served in the Armed Forces during the years of combat and that 189 had lost their lives. It was a sobering number, and it rekindled a desire expressed by University authorities in the early years of the war for a tangible tribute to those members of the Queen's community who had fought and died in the worldwide conflict. After considering first a chapel and then a formal monument, most Queen's officials settled on the idea of a student union building. To commemorate the dead, they would build a place for meeting and conversation, for eating and sleeping; in short, a place where life would go on.

Begun in 1927 on land purchased from the Orphans' Home and Widows' Friend Society of Kingston, the original Students' Memorial Union was officially opened two years later. The finished building contained not only a kitchen, a cafeteria and a tuck shop but also a large open common room overlooked by a billiards area. In the basement were offices for student organizations, including the Canadian Officers' Training Corps, the *Queen's Journal* and the Athletic Board of Control. And at the rear of the building, opening off the landing between the second and third floors, was the Memorial Room, a handsome reading room where photographs of those who had died in the war lined the walls.

In subsequent years, the immense popularity of the Students' Memorial Union created its own problems. The very sense of community that had informed the decision to build the Union in the first place became a flourishing reality in very short order. In less than a decade, the demands being made on this hub of activity were straining its facilities to the breaking point, and grandiose plans for additions and expansion were commissioned from its architects. Another World War interrupted those visions, however. And sadly, the original building — a stately limestone with wide sweeping stairs at one end and a square stone tower at the other — was destroyed by fire in 1947.

Pioneer Broadcasters

It began as an experiment by Queen's electrical engineering students under federal experimental licence 9BT, and some claim that its first broadcast, in 1922, was of a cornet solo played by an engineering student. It was, depending on your source, the first, or at least one of the first, radio stations in the country and among the first in the world. Over the next 20 years, CFRC went through six different transmitters, each built by students and staff and each an improvement on the one before.

Between 1936 and 1942, the University embarked on a commercial-broadcasting venture in partnership with the Kingston *Whig-Standard*. During the 1930s, no other radio station served the Kingston area, and none of the stations in neighbouring cities provided a clear, consistent signal. With the formation of the Canadian Radio Broadcasting Commission (CRBC), however, CFRC became the perfect candidate to expand into a full-time local voice by combining its own programming with that of the CRBC network service. While *The Whig-Standard* undertook to supervise the advertising and office work, the University provided both the on-air personnel and the technical expertise necessary to maintain the equipment.

For six years, the arrangement operated smoothly. In 1942, however, the two partners agreed to go their separate ways; Queen's was more than content to distance itself from the advertising component of commercial radio. (It is easy in retrospect to imagine the medical faculty's consternation over the patent-medicine commercials that were being aired.)

In the late 1960s, CFRC began fund raising and lobbying for permission to establish proper stereo radio facilities. It proved to be one of the longer fights for financing in the history of campus activities. With estimates increasing each year and the necessary resources remaining just out of reach, the "Go Stereo Campaign," as it was dubbed in 1980, became a perennial phenomenon despite a generous contribution in 1976 from Kathleen (Whitton) Ryan (Arts '26), whose husband Frank Ryan (Arts '27) established Ottawa's station CFRA and had begun his career as a broadcaster on the campus airwaves. Champagne brunches, telethons and even a 1982 student fee increase were not quite enough to take the campaign over the top. Five active generations of CFRC Radio Club undergraduates fuelled by an infectious determination and a refusal to accept defeat finally won out, however. In February 1990, stereo broadcasting finally began from an off-campus transmitter located at Kingston Mills, a few miles north of the city.

Student broadcaster, Fleming Hall, 1930

Untamed Radio Waves

Although the electrical engineers at Queen's in the 1920s literally built the campus radio station with their own hands, members of the same faculty in later years came to rue the day that CFRC went on the air. Powerful transmitters on the top floor of Fleming Hall became a serious source of interference for the sensitive experiments often being conducted below. Some nights, procedures had to be held up until 2 a.m., after the broadcasters had signed off. The signal beaming from above also wielded a mysterious influence over the faculty's first computer, at times preventing operators from logging on and at other times apparently making it impossible for them to log off until the radio signal ceased. Even after the faculty was moved to new quarters in 1988 and Fleming Hall became an administrative building, the signal sometimes managed to pop up in unexpected places, occasionally transforming telephones into hand-held radio receivers.

CFRC, Queen's voice since 1922

The Home Boy

Although several of Adam Shortt's protégés and intellectual descendants made their mark on federal government, Duncan McArthur dedicated his talents to his home province of Ontario. A medal-winning history, philosophy and political science student, McArthur graduated from Queen's with a master's degree in 1908. After a tutorial fellowship at Queen's in history, he moved on to the Dominion Archives, where he collaborated with Shortt and A.G. Doughty in the publication of documents relating to constitutional history.

Like many talented scholars, McArthur moved in and out of academe. He trained as a lawyer and was called to the bar in 1915. He served as the general manager of a trust company from 1919 to 1922, and then in 1922, he returned to Queen's as the head of the department of history, a position he held for 12 years. A tribute by Professor A.E. Prince later recalled him as an inspiring man whose classroom expositions "were salted with a whimsical, dry humour and garnished with apt anecdotes of men and affairs."

Upon leaving Queen's, the popular professor found a wider application for his talents. In 1934, he accepted the position of Deputy Minister of Education for the province, and six years later, in an unusual political move, he was promoted to full minister and took up a seat in the legislature. McArthur completely overhauled the educational process in Ontario. After personal investigations across the country and in Britain and Scandinavia, he set about streamlining the system, building in flexibility and a new emphasis on music and art. Postwar students in the modernized education system of Ontario owe much to the policies shaped by this student and professor from the university at Kingston.

At Queen's, in honour of his accomplishments, the Faculty of Education on West Campus is housed in the Duncan McArthur College of Education.

McArthur's buddy system: investing in the future

Students studying near end of term, Douglas Library

Student Strikes

The student strike of 1928 followed three separate rulings by the Senate on matters of student conduct: an assault; a drinking contest that landed both participants in hospital; and a dance hosted by three students who circumvented the strict letter of a Senate decision forbidding the event. The drinkers and the dancers had all been suspended, and at a mass meeting of the Alma Mater Society on March 22, students voted to go on strike until the Senate reconsidered its position.

The Senate's authority and concern for the good reputation of the University collided with the students' insistence on their right to self-government and off-campus privacy. In the words of Queen's historian F.W. Gibson, "Each side supported its stand by reference to large principles." In the end, only the intervention of the newly formed Alumni Association, in the person of its president, R.O. Sweezey, convinced the students to return to classes.

The conflict was never clearly resolved, but it did have at least one important consequence. Many Trustees, ignoring the issues involved, laid responsibility for the debacle at the feet of Principal R. Bruce Taylor, suggesting that he was personally responsible for allowing the situation to slip from his control. The Board of Trustees allowed a year to pass, then approached Taylor and requested his resignation.

The precedent for the student strike of 1928 had been a feeble protest half a century earlier. At a time when attendance at morning chapel service was a compulsory beginning to each student's day, it was not surprising that two young men found drunk in a hallway outside class were promptly expelled. A student petition failed to secure a reprieve for the guilty parties, and students tried to reinforce their stand with a one-day strike. When the Senate threatened to expel anyone absent from classes for any reason other than illness, the students abruptly reconsidered the wisdom of their position; eight wrote letters of apology to the Senate for good measure.

"The miasma of industrial commerce
has soiled the face of many academies."
— Hamilton Fyfe, from his final report, 1935-36

Hamilton Fyfe (1930-36): A Classicist's Depression

Fond of joking that he "came with the Depression," William Hamilton Fyfe, Principal from 1930 to 1936, had the unfortunate honour of presiding over Queen's during some of the University's bleakest financial years. Witty, articulate and a good public speaker, Fyfe had a reputation as a man who "scorned the pompous and hollow." His ambitions for Queen's were ultimately thwarted, not simply by the times but perhaps by the University itself.

Fyfe the orator made clear his plans for change at Queen's. "The horizon of the typical undergraduate student is said to be bounded by the lectures, examinations, dances, films and gladiatorial games at which he is a frenzied spectator," he said. "I am not without hope that this familiar portrait may become, before long, a caricature." Alas, although reputedly able to translate the morning newspaper into Latin and Greek as mental exercise, Fyfe the administrator and educator made few inroads before resigning in frustration.

Fyfe's dream of reaffirming classical scholarly values ran headlong into both economic reality and the sense of pessimism that permeated the campus during those difficult times. He managed to restore faculty confidence in the Principal's academic leadership by bringing both resident artist Goodridge Roberts and resident musician Frank L. Harrison to Queen's. But Fyfe, too, seemed gradually to lose hope. He was known to remark that "a student seeking a pass B.A. need do little more than register and grow older." Of Queen's in general, the Principal concluded that "education here is only a rumour." And he summarized his opinion of the conversational skills of Kingstonians by commenting that he would remember the city as the place where "the weather is always 'unusual' for this time of year."

Fyfe went on to distinguish himself as Principal of Scotland's University of Aberdeen. While Queen's took pride in this connection, doubtless many on campus were relieved to see him go.

Practice, Harrison-LeCaine Hall, built 1974

Agnes Etherington Art Centre

The Agnes Etherington Art Centre opened its doors on October 12, 1957. Mrs. Agnes Etherington, sister of both Chancellor James Richardson and George Taylor Richardson, for whom the stadium was named, bequeathed her own home to the University "for the furtherance of art and music and for the exhibition of pictures and music and not for use as a residence." (Several former homes in the area had been taken over for student housing.)

Etherington's donation was not an isolated act of generosity. Born into one of Queen's leading families, she had been the founding president of the Kingston Art and Music Association. In addition, as an administrator of the George Taylor Richardson Memorial Fund, she provided crucial financial support for the earliest art programmes at Queen's. It was through her efforts that artist André Biéler came to Queen's, and she convinced the Faculty of Arts that an art course for university students, given by a qualified resident artist, should count as a degree credit.

Artist on Campus

A significant artist in his own right and one with an international profile, Swiss-born André Biéler also painted on the living canvas of Queen's University. In the years following his arrival at Queen's in the summer of 1936, he gave the first lectures on the history and appreciation of art. Providing studio instruction and supervising citywide juried exhibitions, he even broadcast a series of radio talks over Queen's radio station, CFRC. Out of his boundless enthusiasm and creativity, art education at Queen's was born.

A home for art

Fine Arts student, Ontario Hall

They have marched in Texas, Florida, Winnipeg and, closer to home, in Toronto, Montreal and London. They have split the autumn air of countless football afternoons and lightened the steps of generations of Queen's students on parade. Along with Queen's cheerleaders, Highland dancers and drum majorettes, they share the rare distinction of having incited more yelling, stomping, whistling, waving, jumping and general tomfoolery than any other institution in the University's history. And if they themselves have not actually stolen any goalposts from rival campuses, they have at least seen it done . . . more than once. They are the Queen's Bands — the Brass Band, established in 1905, and the Pipe Band, established in 1924 — and every Queen's student, without exception, has heard them play, if only in the distance, the drums thumping or the song of the pipes borne on the campus air.

The Queen's University Pipe Band first set the tricolour to music in 1925

Their regalia has ranged from the tatty to the truly impressive, from white ducks and tricoloured sweaters to the grand Royal Stuart tartan. At times, they have appeared better — at least more extraordinarily — equipped than the football players they accompanied, and even a partial list of their raiment through the years is truly wondrous to read: belts and buckles, white spats, plaids, kilts, glengarry bonnets, tams, Air Force battle-dress jackets, gauntlets, garters, hose tabs, badges, balmorals, sporrans and cairngorms.

The Queen's Bands have always made an impressive sound and have almost always been an impressive sight to behold. In its 75th-anniversary book, *Queen's Bands 1905-1980*, Chancellor Emeritus John Stirling, a founding member of the Brass Band, described the original group of 12 young freshmen as ragged enthusiasts with a repertoire limited to the Queen's College colours and a couple of John Philip Sousa marches, and while they did not have uniforms, there was humour to take the place of precision in their visual impact, for as they stepped merrily along in formation, they were brought up in the rear by ''Stirling, 6'1'', playing the bass drum and, beside him, Shortie Orwell, 4'11'', playing the kettledrum.''

Face paint is optional

In a strange way, football finally laid to rest the issue of fraternities at Queen's. Greek-letter organizations, as they were called, had sparked a heated and persistent debate. The issue eventually held centre stage during the Alma Mater Society (AMS) election in the fall of 1933, which was won by the Arts-Levana-Theology party on an antifraternity platform. And finally, the whole fuss triggered one of the harshest and most controversial AMS Court decisions ever made. Yet symbolically and emotionally, the fraternities died only a year later, when the Queen's football team of 1934, dubbed the "Fearless Fourteen," won the intercollegiate championship.

No mere tempest in a teapot, the question of fraternities on campus touched a very sensitive nerve among Queen's people. Quite simply, most students and alumni took offence at the suggestion that within the close-knit community, a small confraternity of friends was necessary for mutual support and companionship. Further, they viewed the allegiance of such groups to larger national and international organizations as a direct attack on the spirit and loyalty that joined together all members of the University.

After years of escalating debate, which had begun in the early 1920s, the issue devolved into a series of AMS constitutional wrangles that first banned the groups, then allowed them, then banned them once more. After a last flurry of committee work and compromise, peace finally descended on the battle of the secret societies in the spring term of 1934. It lasted for only a matter of days. Two days after the medical school's convocation, the medical students' Psi Delta Phi, the last lingering Greek-letter society on campus, pushed the AMS too far by becoming the Beta Sigma Chapter of an international medical fraternity, Nu Sigma Nu.

Along with nine professors who also pledged as members, the medical students deliberately flouted the careful collective agreement, and with the resumption of classes in the fall, a brief and fierce battle took place. The 24 fraternity members were called before an AMS Court composed of three judges, a sheriff, a chief of police, a Court clerk, a prosecuting attorney, a defence counsel, a "crier" and 800 spectators. When the Court refused their request for more time to prepare a defence — they had received only one day's notice — the defen-

dants marched out and were thereupon found guilty of contempt of Court. In absentia, the Court also convicted each of them of contravening the AMS constitution and assigned a bitter punishment: suspension from all student political, athletic and social activities for one academic year.

With that, the University held its breath. And so did much of the Canadian sports world, for among the guilty were four members of the Queen's senior football team. Suddenly, the issue of fraternities had jeopardized what many were already convinced was a potential championship season. In the days that followed, the mixture of sports fever and campus politics proved a heady concoction. Observers speculated that even if the AMS did not back down, student opinion would simply reverse itself, especially if Queen's lost the next scheduled game against a strong Toronto team. Some even muttered demands for a plebiscite, and accusing fingers pointed at the AMS Court and the executive responsible for bringing matters to such a pass.

The student government stood firm, however, and soon gained the staunch support of the Athletic Board of Control — as well as the Senate and the Board of Trustees — which upheld the decision barring the fraternity brothers from playing. When the team won its next outing, tensions eased considerably, as if victory somehow vindicated the suspensions. Yet many reserved judgment. The surviving players — the Fearless Fourteen — struggled on through the season, losing only twice and finishing the year tied for the lead with Toronto. With the end of the season, the fate of fraternities at Queen's was left utterly tangled up in the fortunes of this short-handed team and the serendipitous outcome of one final game. When Queen's defeated Toronto 8 to 7 in the title game, two things happened: the team made headlines across the country (a poll conducted by the Canadian Press voted its success the most thrilling sports moment of 1934), and the victory settled the question of fraternities for good.

In the years since, the Senate has reaffirmed the AMS decision, quoting its own position in the annual University calendar: "By resolution of Senate, no student registered at Queen's University may form or become a member of any chapter of any externally affiliated fraternity or sorority at or near Kingston."

"Wherever Queen's men be:
It's Queen's for all and all for Queen's.
That's true Fraternity."
— *The Queen's Review*, 1934

During his tenure as Principal of Queen's, Robert C. Wallace guided the University through years of economic depression, a world war and the postwar wave of returning veterans. They were times of turmoil and pending change, in which the sense of the day was inevitably informed by the fear or eager anticipation of tomorrow. It was also a time of bombast and confusion; Principal Wallace, in contrast to the age, stuck to simple truths and articulated them with such eloquence and conviction that he earned the devoted support of a whole generation.

Born in the Orkney Islands, Wallace received his education in Scotland and in Europe. He taught geology at the University of Manitoba from 1912 to 1928 and served as president of the University of Alberta from 1928 to 1936, during which time he founded what is now known as the Banff School of Fine Arts. Arriving at Queen's in 1936, during the Depression, Wallace helped to combat the creeping pessimism that had come with years of underfunding. By the time war broke out, the University stood ready to accommodate a flood of new demands from government and the military.

A shrewd administrator, with the talent and character necessary to ensure that the school's war efforts did not threaten its survival, Wallace was also the University's spiritual guide during the years of conflict. He dedicated the University to the business of warfare, but there was none of the hawkish rhetoric that had attended Queen's involvement during World War I. People knew what horrors to expect from the fighting, and at home, Wallace spoke often to students about their privileged position and of their responsibility to acquire the skills necessary to contribute effectively to the war effort.

Following the war, and until his retirement in 1951, Wallace was the first in a series of Queen's principals to be faced with the problems of explosive growth. Freed of wartime demands, the University expanded in all directions as a wave of veterans made their way through the system and out into the booming postwar society.

In the summer of 1937, Colonel R.S. McLaughlin, president of General Motors of Canada, turned down a request to assist the new Industrial Relations Centre at Queen's. His impatient comment was "too much theory and too little practical sense," a response that was to change dramatically in the years to come. A great admirer of Principal Robert C. Wallace and a friend of Chancellor C.A. Dunning, McLaughlin became one of Queen's greatest benefactors. McLaughlin Hall, the R. Samuel McLaughlin Fellowships, the McLaughlin Trust and the McLaughlin Research Chairs are all named in his honour, and the women's residence, Adelaide Hall, is named for Adelaide McLaughlin, whose generosity made it possible. One of the few strings ever attached to the McLaughlins' generous assistance followed the destruction by fire of the Students' Memorial Union Building in 1947. The Colonel's support for reconstruction was contingent upon the Great Hall of the new building being renamed Wallace Hall.

Principal Robert C. Wallace

In 1938, Queen's counted only 1,800 full-time students, and the City of Kingston held no more than 23,000 people. It was a small community, removed from the mainstream during a humbling time of economic depression. Yet in August of that year, U.S. President Franklin Delano Roosevelt accepted an honorary degree from Queen's University at a special open-air convocation and, in his address, which was broadcast worldwide, made the deliberate declaration that, for a fiery moment, placed Kingston and the University under the spotlight of world attention. ''The Dominion of Canada is part of the sisterhood of the British Empire,'' Roosevelt said. ''I give to you assurance that the people of the United States will not stand idly by if domination of Canadian soil is threatened by any other Empire.''

Viewed through the historical lens of the war that followed, the depth of isolationist sentiment in the United States in 1938 is impossible to appreciate. Americans did not want any part of a European war. Even as Roosevelt perceived the inevitability of international conflict, he remained tied by the realities of American domestic politics, and as the world political situation bent under pressure from central Europe, people watched for the slightest suggestion that America would intervene. Roosevelt's speech from the playing field of the George Taylor Richardson Memorial Stadium —containing, as it did, an ambiguous suggestion of threats and domination and of empires jostling —therefore received rapt attention around the world. Delivered on Canadian soil, it was possible to interpret it at face value as simply the reassuring declaration of a powerful nation's commitment to its neighbour. Yet many heard much more in it than that, and in a letter to Canada's Governor General, Lord Tweedsmuir, Roosevelt himself declared that the occasion, among other things, did seem ''to fit in with the Hitler situation and had, I hope, some small effect on Berlin.''

''I am going to do what I very seldom do. I will write my name in full.''

— Franklin Delano Roosevelt, on signing *The Domesday Book*, August 18, 1938

World War II precipitated a number of changes at Queen's, creating trends that survived the end of hostilities. Modern warfare meant ever-increasing demands for trained technical personnel, and Queen's expanded its commitment to the practical sciences. In addition, women found a wider scope for their talents and the Faculty of Applied Science responded by expanding dramatically. In 1942, the University created the degree programme in nursing science, and as the number of engineering students rose, the faculty accepted its first women students. A year later, the Faculty of Medicine — equally pressed to produce qualified personnel — accepted women once again. As Principal Robert C. Wallace reminded students, war in the 1940s had become a complicated and technical business. Duty to one's country, for women and for men, often meant staying in school and getting an education.

Science class of 1943

''And We do further Will, Ordain and
Appoint that no religious test or
qualification shall be required . . . ''
— Royal Charter, Queen's College

Closed Doors

"Contrary to newspaper reports, no Japanese students have been admitted to Queen's this session. One Canadian-born student of Japanese parentage, who was admitted in 1940 and who had completed his second year in Applied Science and whose loyalty was proved, has been allowed to continue his course. He is the only Japanese in attendance."
— *The Queen's Review*, October 1942

Campus posters

The Denominational Test

Amidst the heroism and self-sacrifice of the war effort at Queen's, the minutes of the Board of Trustees' meetings record a less worthy episode. Between 1942 and 1945, an ongoing discussion took place concerning what was termed the "Jewish problem" at Queen's University. The issue revolved around the fact that a small but growing number of students at Queen's were Jewish Montrealers. The University's Principal, Vice-Principal, Board of Trustees and a special select committee dedicated a discomfiting amount of time and thought to the question of how to solve the "problem." To its credit, the University finally remembered its long-standing tradition. In its Royal Charter of 1841, Queen's had made it clear that there was no denominational test for students who wished to attend. Anti-Semitism eventually encountered a deep-seated abhorrence of discrimination that succeeded in bringing the entire discussion to an end. All involved finally agreed with Professor H.L. Tracy of the classics department, who from the outset had been the sole voice in the Senate to insist that "the whole question should be dropped."

In Memoriam

The Principal's Report of 1945-46 records "that there were 2,917 graduates and former students in the various services and that 157 were killed in action, died in active service or were officially presumed dead. Two hundred and sixty-eight honours and distinctions were awarded, including the Victoria Cross won by Major John Weir Foote, Arts '33, of the Canadian Chaplain Service."

The 1945 *Tricolour*, the student yearbook, included a list of those killed in action or those who had died in active service between 1939 and 1945.

In the end, 168 names were inscribed on a brass plaque that is mounted in the Memorial Room of the John Deutsch University Centre.

AMS executive, 1989-90; Memorial Room

Queen's Theological Hall, third oldest building on campus; completed in 1880

Christmas of 1947

On December 22, 1947, Grant Hall was the scene of a unique Christmas party. The University, so long accustomed to its parental role in the lives of students, discovered that it had also become a grandparent. That year, 1,756 veterans attended classes; 556 of them were married, and they had a total of 362 children. All were invited to a Yuletide celebration.

More than 160 stockings stuffed by alumnae from the Kingston area were distributed to the children. "Santa Claus materialized out of thin air, with the aid of magician Michael Roth (Arts '48)." Movies were shown, and the Queen's University Pipe Band entertained with music and dancing. The party — organized by the newly appointed Chaplain, A.M. Laverty — opened with a short message from Principal Robert C. Wallace intended to underline the respect that had prompted the gathering. "We realize," he told the young parents, "that things are not easy for you in many cases, and we admire your courage in keeping up this life at the University."

An article from the April 1950 *Queen's Review* by Padre A.M. Laverty provides an even more striking description of the "new look" on campus:

"As it has to all colleges, the 'New Look' in student bodies has come to Queen's in these postwar years. Side by side with the fuzzy-cheeked crop of recent high school graduates sit men who remember vividly the North Atlantic convoy, the Caen-Falaise road and the Ruhr run. While one comes to classes hoping for a 10 o'clock coffee date with his choice-of-the-moment, another is hoping that his 2-year-old son will soon get over his habit of waking before 6:00 in the morning. While one schemes how to stretch his weekly allowance to include a weekend of skiing in northern New York, another is figuring how to pay the family milk bill on a Department of Veteran Affairs allowance and his summer savings."

The Padre

In 1947, Principal Robert C. Wallace, describing the Chaplain's office, explained that "his work will be as he finds it and makes it." According to the Principal, all the University required of the newly hired Reverend A.M. Laverty was that he "be helpful."

The Padre, as Queen's students fondly knew him over the next four decades, proved to have surpassing talent for the job. Initially, he counselled returning veterans, who had grown accustomed to having a military chaplain with whom to talk. Later, generations of fresh-faced high school graduates entering the University found their way to his office, and Padre Laverty brought a profound meaning to the task of simply being helpful.

In 1946, the University spilled over with new students and veterans, completely overwhelming the limited campus residence facilities and the city's rooming houses. Many new students, arriving in the city to register, spent their first nights on cots in the gymnasium. If they failed to find rental accommodation, the University helped with placements in a variety of former military barracks and in the so-called Stone Frigate, an unused cadets' facility at the Royal Military College.

The Aluminum Company of Canada made space available in the hutments built during the war for employees of its expanded Kingston facilities; 140 single students and 80 married men with families set up there. The University even hosted a small trailer-park community with half a dozen portable homes parked behind the gymnasium, which served as their source of water and electricity.

No solution went untried. Harry Pyke (B.Sc. '50) of South Porcupine, Ontario, and Raymond Desjardins (B.Sc. '50) of Calgary, Alberta, both Royal Canadian Air Force veterans with families, even built their own six-room house on land purchased from the City of Kingston. Jack Taylor of Port Hope, Ontario — another self-sufficient Air Force veteran — bedded down for the winter of that crowded school year on his 35-foot schooner, *Hamish*, sailed by Taylor from Lunenburg, Nova Scotia, where it had once served as a part of the Maritime fishing fleet.

Padre A.M. Laverty, Grant Hall

Biology greenhouse, roof of Earl Hall

"Our Botanical Garden is making progress."

— George Lawson, Queen's first natural history professor, 1863

The search for knowledge sometimes takes precedence over human comfort. When Queen's established the Biological Field Station in 1945 on a scenic peninsula jutting out into Lake Opinicon, north of Kingston, the price of enlightenment was paid by those using the living accommodations. The station's original facilities provided a curious study in contrasts.

Along with 11 rudimentary two-bunk cabins and a three-bedroom director's cottage, the station consisted of a large central lodge for cooking, eating and relaxing. At the waterfront, a two-storey boathouse contained a workshop next to the boat slips and a classroom above. Water at the lodge came from an outdoor pump, and a wood stove, which also heated the water for washing dishes, was used for cooking. No hot water was available for personal use, and a flush toilet remained a distant dream. In short, life at Opinicon came with all of the rough-hewn pleasures of camping and cottaging.

The laboratory building, on the other hand, was the jewel in the crown of the Opinicon station. It boasted hot and cold running water, fluorescent lights, electric outlets within easy reach and propane gas and compressed air. A walk-in refrigerator kept certain specimens cool, while a walk-in incubator kept others warm. Though not commonplace at an outpost research station, the wealth of equipment reflected the Queen's department of biology's preference for methods that emphasized appreciating the environment as a whole by first isolating and understanding its parts. Primitive lodgings meant nothing weighed against the ability to take that curiosity to the field.

Throughout its history, the Queen's University Biological Field Station has remained an unlimited resource, open for use in as many ways as curiosity can devise. Queen's biologists and visiting biologists have pursued studies in forestry and soils, entomology, botany, limnology, avian ecology and even "mouse colonization of island habitats."

Both living space and new laboratories at the station have kept pace with changing needs, despite such setbacks as a 1979 tornado that necessitated the replacement of cabins. More important, the station has grown in size — from 45 acres to almost 3,000 acres. That land, which includes miles of waterfront secured in 1989, serves to protect the station from the encroaching community of cottages and has provided new areas of pasture, old forest, second-growth foliage and undisturbed shoreline for controlled study. As the years pass, the property guards the future of the station's greatest treasure, its long-standing and ever-growing pool of statistics, information culled from Queen's own carefully watched wilderness world.

Locust-control experiment

Autumn midday, Ontario Hall

In its Friday, September 11, 1987, edition, the *Queen's Journal* reported that at a special meeting, the Board of Trustees voted 19 to 5 in favour of completely divesting itself of its shares in companies with connections to South Africa. The decision capped a 10-year debate on campus over the ethics of doing business with a country governed by racist policies, a debate that twice led to the storming of a Board of Trustees' meeting by student and faculty protesters. Sustained by widespread pressure from within the University community, the controversy eventually led to a crucial faculty vote in May 1987. With nearly 60 percent of the responding faculty in favour of divestment, the Board's Committee on Social Responsibility recommended selling off $16.5 millon worth of shares in a number of companies. The move dramatically overturned an October 1986 decision that favoured only limited divestment.

The Chancellor Dunning Trust: A Renewable Gift

Over the course of the University's history, a great variety of lectureships and visitorships have been established, ranging in topic from legal philosophy to plant physiology. They sometimes represent vast sums of money and sometimes more modest amounts, but almost always, they commemorate and celebrate the convictions, interests and visions of individuals who played a significant role in the University's life. Each keeps alive a voice in the conversations of learning at Queen's. One of the most prestigious is the Chancellor Dunning Trust, which was set up by an anonymous donor:

"To the Principal and Vice-Chancellor of Queen's University, I desire to establish at Queen's University a permanent tribute to your Chancellor, Honourable Charles A. Dunning, in the hope that the inspiration of a life of public service will help future students to do their part in service to humanity.

"To this end, I am enclosing a cheque for $100,000 payable to 'Queen's University Endowment Fund' and request that the University accept the following obligations with regard thereto:
1. That the donation shall be treated with absolute confidence as anonymous;
2. That it be called the 'Chancellor Dunning Trust';
3. That once in every three years, the Trustees of Queen's University read this letter and decide, in the light of the then existing conditions, how best the income from the Trust may be expended to promote understanding and appreciation of the supreme importance of the dignity, freedom and responsibility of the individual person in human society and shall publish this memorandum, together with their decision, in the Students' newspaper."
— Anonymous Friend of Chancellor Dunning, October 2, 1946

Relaxing between classes

Adding Substance to Ceremony

The office of Rector at Queen's demonstrates the sometimes peculiar ways of political office and the evolution of power. Conceived as a largely ceremonial office patterned on the rectorships of Scottish universities, the Rector originally served as the nominal representative of students on the Board of Trustees. Although the Rector was elected every three years by the students themselves, the position was such that it did not originally require the incumbent to have a residence in Kingston. The first Rector, Reverend Samuel Dyde, 1913-16, lived in Alberta throughout his tenure.

With the exception of James L. Robertson, a noted agriculturist who succeeded Dyde after winning an election against Sir John M. Gibson, former Lieutenant Governor of Ontario, the Rector was always elected by acclamation. In other words, even the elections were ceremonial, and although there were some outstanding Rectors, including B.K. Sandwell and Norman Rogers, all that was really expected of the incumbent was a rectorial address — sometimes two — given during his period in office. All that changed, however, with the arrival of Leonard Brockington.

Considered to be the greatest of Queen's Rectors, Brockington transformed the job from a nominal honour on paper only to an honourable occupation. A famed orator, Brockington came to Queen's in 1947 to deliver the Alma Mater Society lecture and made such an impression that by the end of the year, the students prevailed upon him to become Rector. Every three years until his death 19 years later, the students reaffirmed their high estimation. In return, this very successful and influential man made Queen's one of his life's central concerns, a responsibility which he took seriously and which served as an obvious source of delight to him.

Brockington made it his business to attend not only Board meetings but convocations and other official functions as well. He shed the light of his influence on the University in numerous unusual ways, by convincing his friends—Nicholas Monsarrat, Yousuf Karsh and Lord and Lady Tweedsmuir, among others—to visit the campus or to make donations of time, money, manuscripts and artifacts to the University community.

Brockington belonged to an age that still delighted in oratory, and he could stir the soul of any audience. His wartime radio broadcasts from Britain were carried throughout the Allied world. A "master of all the skills of the spoken word," he was described by *The Globe and Mail* as "Churchillian" — although it might be noted that while Churchill's speeches were often written out as a free-form poetry of timing and pauses, Brockington rarely had more than jottings and headings to prompt him. Even in conversation, his remarkable memory held a story for every occasion. In later years, he liked to say he was between his dotage and his anecdotage.

Brockington's active role as Rector had radically altered the perception of the office, and although he was succeeded by Canadian Senator M. Grattan O'Leary, Queen's students, who already had seats on the Senate, began campaigning only a year later for representation on the Board of Trustees. Brockington had shown them how useful such influence could be. They displaced their elected Rector and insisted that a student be given the job. R. Alan Broadbent became the first of the new breed of Rector, but even as he took up his responsibilities in the modern office of campus ombudsman, he filled a vacancy left by a man who had transformed the rectorship from a ceremonial function into a task of substance.

Leonard Brockington

Night view on University Avenue

Football crowd, Alumni Weekend

For many students and alumni, the names Jimmy Bews and Frank Tindall are synonymous with athletics at Queen's. Frank Tindall Field, the busiest outdoor sporting area on campus, commemorates the man who coached football and basketball at Queen's from 1947 until 1975; the BEWS Intramural Sports League — along with WIC (Women's Intramural Committee) and BEWIC (coeducational sports) — is a lively and fitting tribute to James Graham Bews, the first physical director at Queen's. Bews, a former stonemason, made fitness and strenuous physical activity an integral part of life at the University, long before exercise became a fashionable pastime.

Frank Tindall's career at Queen's began with a short-lived stint in 1939 when the All-American football player arrived from Syracuse, New York, to take over the duties of football coach. During that year, his Gaels had a 3-3 record. The following year, war interrupted the University's intercollegiate sports programme, and Tindall and the University temporarily parted company. He returned in 1947 and stayed until his retirement in 1975. According to the *Queen's Alumni Review* of January/February 1976, his football career totals showed 111 games won against 84 losses and 2 ties. His teams outscored their opponents 3,572 to 2,972. With Tindall at the helm during the remarkable 1960s, the Gaels won the Yates Cup five times and the Vanier Cup once and were runners-up in the other seasons.

Coach Frank Tindall

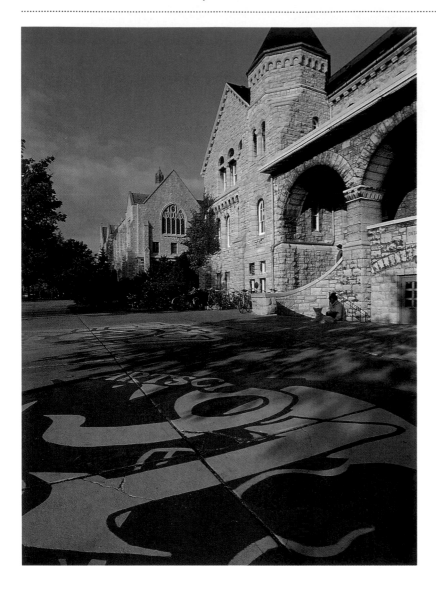

"Though of the Class of Arts '91, a change of course left me at Queen's in the autumn of 1891. The adoption of a yell was being urged. I favoured Gaelic because of Queen's founders and traditions. The Alma Mater Society appointed a committee. I was asked to formulate a Gaelic yell. I decided on 'Red, blue and yellow. Queen's forever!' in Gaelic, followed by an authentic Scottish war cry. Two Gaels, F.A. McRae and D. Cameron, did the translating for me. I got another Gael called McLean to read me a list of Scottish war cries. When he came to *Cha Gheill!* I stopped him.

" 'What does that mean?'

" '*Nil desperandum*,' he replied. The resulting yell was as follows:

" 'Queen's! *Dearg, gor'mus, buidthe!/Oil-thigh na Banrighinn gu brath!/Cha Gheill! Cha Gheill! Cha Gheill!*'

"Translation:

Red! Blue! Yellow! / Queen's forever! / No surrender!

"Pronunciation (as well as a non-Gael can give it): Jarg, gormoos, boo-e-e-e (this last word drawn out on a rising note like a war whoop) Oil tye na vanree gu brath / Hah Yale (or Yile)!

"Both *Cha* and *Gheill* should be emphasized. *Cha* should be one beat; *Gheill* should have two. It should be given as a clan would yell it when foes attacked them. It is an actual war cry heard many a time in the glens long ago.

"This yell was adopted by the committee October 9 and by the AMS October 10, 1891. On October 24 (I was not present), the AMS changed it.

"The Gaels took little interest, being horrified by our mispronunciation and profanation of the language of the Garden of Eden.

"This change cut out what to me was the best part of the yell — 'Red, blue and yellow.' People living on Union Street told me that when the first yell was given October 10 by students coming north after the AMS meeting, the wild shriek of the *Dearg, gor'mus, buidthe*! was by far the most fearsome part and carried farther.

"The yell as changed October 24, 1891, is the one used ever since, though often fearfully mispronounced and with wrong tempo."

— Alfred E. Lavell, Toronto, September 15, 1948

"Cha Gheill! Cha Gheill! Cha Gheill!"

Future Health

In 1939, Marion Ross, physical director for women, submitted her official report to the Principal. In it, she noted her department's "increased emphasis on the value of conscious physical development in order to ensure future healthy living." She explained that "the repeated 'doing' of an exercise is not considered sufficient but requires the understanding by the student of the necessity for exercise in the development of a healthy body. . . . An effort is made to have the students learn sports which they will follow after they leave college to conserve their own fitness."

The balanced tone of Ross's report found expression in the next half-century of growth in women's athletics at Queen's. By the late 1980s, Queen's possessed not only strong women's varsity teams but, even more important, an impressively active intramural system designed to include fun and competition and to provide another of Ross's simple prescriptions: "sufficient skill to enjoy further participation."

Racing sculls, end of season

During the 1950s and 1960s, women in athletics at Queen's joked that all of women's sports at the University operated on a budget smaller than the football team's dry-cleaning bill. They were not exaggerating by much. Nonetheless, women's inter-university teams grew in size, won their share of glory and sometimes surpassed the men. By the late 1980s, they accounted for fully half the competitive teams at Queen's. In 1989, women's teams represented Queen's in all 21 OWIAA (Ontario Women's Interuniversity Athletic Association) sports: badminton, basketball, curling, diving, fencing, field hockey, figure skating, gymnastics, hockey, rowing, alpine skiing, Nordic skiing, soccer, squash, swimming, synchronized swimming, tennis, cross-country, track and field, volleyball and water polo.

In the 1980s, the Queen's soccer team became a proud symbol of advances in women's competitive athletics. Founded in 1977 by Queen's soccer pioneer Sue Hofman, the team went from being one without a league to being OWIAA- and CIAU (Canadian Interuniversity Athletic Union)-sanctioned champion in only 12 years. At the same time, Queen's interuniversity coordinator Professor Anne Turnbull helped the team translate its search for uniforms into a successful quest for trophies.

Women's indoor soccer

The third verse of *Queen's College Colours* exhorts students to "remember Captain Curtis and the conquerors of Yale," a reference to Queen's 3-0 hockey victory over Yale University in New York City in 1897. One of those conquerors was 23-year-old John Joseph (Jock) Harty, and although his teammates' names have faded from memory, his has not. As a reminder, there has been a Jock Harty Arena at Queen's since 1922.

The original Jock Harty Memorial Arena was erected as a tribute to the man who, although a qualified medical doctor and later an executive of the Canadian Locomotive Company Limited, saved his greatest enthusiasm for the game of hockey. As player and coach, he maintained his connection with the game and with Queen's from his youth — when he "could manipulate the puck in less space and dodge more rapidly than any other player" — until his death at 44 from pneumonia in postwar Britain.

The memorial arena, located just off Union Street, burned down after only two years. It was rebuilt on Arch Street, and for the next 33 years, the "Jock Harty" served both the city and the University before being torn down to make way for campus expansion. In 1970, Jock Harty Arena, in its third incarnation, opened as part of the new Queen's Physical Education Centre.

Registering students pass through Jock Harty Arena each fall

For All Occasions

Jock Harty Arena serves in a variety of other essential capacities. For many students, it is the building through which they enter Queen's when they register in first year, and as a convocation hall, it is the building from which they leave the University, with their degrees in hand. During the years between arrival and departure, Jock Harty periodically becomes an unforgettably cavernous examination room, where anxious students toil through Christmas and final exams; on other occasions, its darkened interior becomes an equally memorable concert and dance hall.

Rock climbers scale the walls of Jock Harty Arena

Mackintosh and Corry: Their names have become one word on the lips of thousands of students who have attended Queen's since 1974, when the newest campus building was named in their honour. It is a fitting tribute to the friendship and close working relationship of these two men that it is now difficult to think of one without the other.

The respect that William Archibald Mackintosh and James Alexander Corry had for one another reshaped the most important jobs in the hierarchy of the University's administration. During Mackintosh's term as Principal, Vice-Principal Corry was offered the presidency of the University of Saskatchewan. Given that there was no room for him to advance within the Queen's structure, it seemed likely that he would accept.

Concerned about losing such a valuable adminis-trator and advisor, Mackintosh endorsed a plan devised by Chairman E.C. Gill of the Board of Trustees during the summer of 1958. The title of Vice-Chancellor was to be removed from its traditional place among the duties of the Principal and assigned to Mackintosh, leaving the Principal's job open for Corry. Before the scheme was put into effect, Corry, in fact, had turned down the Saskatchewan job, content to remain in his position as Vice-Principal of Queen's, but Gill and Mackintosh were determined to carry on. The necessary changes to the University's Charter were made by Parliament. The new arrangement went into effect September 1, 1961, and although the process was entirely irregular, the very popular appointment of Alec Corry as the Principal of Queen's University was achieved without the premature loss of W.A. Mackintosh.

Outdoor studies, Mackintosh-Corry Hall

James Alexander Corry (1961-68)

James Alexander Corry, a great theorist and expert in Canadian federalism, once described political studies as a field in which "change was so rapid and so drastic that nothing stayed put long enough to describe it . . . ." And as an administrator, he discovered that the same words applied to the running of a university in the booming years of the 1950s and 60s. While his friend Mackintosh earned the title "The Building Principal" because of the incredible expansion in campus facilities during his tenure, Corry, as Vice-Principal and Mackintosh's close collaborator, played an essential role in ensuring that demands for wider educational opportunities did not tear the school apart.

By the time Corry took over the helm himself in 1961, such growth had become commonplace, and thanks largely to his efforts, fears about changing the heart and soul of the University at Kingston had proved groundless. Nonetheless, the list of changes he then supervised during only seven years in office is staggering. During his first year as Principal, there were 10 percent more students on campus than there had been the previous year, and before his retirement, that number would compound and grow an additional 70 percent. Where once there were 10 students, there were suddenly 18. Curricula that were generations old had to be updated to keep pace with the postwar world. A department of computing science appeared, as did the new School of Rehabilitation Therapy. An Institute of Intergovernmental Relations began systematic studies of the interactions among federal, provincial and municipal governments — a discipline that Corry in his earlier academic life had helped pioneer in Canada. The Duncan McArthur College of Education opened. And, including those under construction at his retirement, the number of residence spaces available for students at Queen's doubled to more than 2,000.

No more explanation is necessary for the unusual title of Chapter VIII of Corry's memoirs: "Principal of Queen's: Running the Rapids."

W.A. Mackintosh (1951-61)

After 20 years as a professor of economics at Queen's, William Archibald Mackintosh moved into wartime service in Ottawa as an assistant to the Deputy Minister of Finance, transferring eventually to the Department of Reconstruction and Supply. The *Winnipeg Free Press* later claimed that "there was, in fact, no aspect of our wartime economic policies in which he was not actively consulted and in which his judgment as a rule was not decisive." Yet Mackintosh's favourite wartime tale, out of all of his experience, involved Queen's, the school he would return to in the postwar years as Dean of Arts, head of economics and political studies and, eventually, Principal.

During the war, Mackintosh's responsibilities required regular flights to London, England, by way of Gander, Newfoundland, where fuel was taken on. One such stopover kept Mackintosh and a planeload of others waiting for hours, frustrated by the security regulations that denied them information about departure time or flight path. As Herb Hamilton, onetime editor of the *Queen's Alumni Review*, recounted the story: "An airman sidled up to Dr. Mackintosh and whispered out of the side of his mouth, 'You will be departing at 1600 hours, you will be flying at a height of 5,000 feet for one hour and then at 20,000 feet for five hours, and the weather outlook is most favourable. *Cha Gheill!*' "

The story of the Queen's department of film studies had its unlikely beginning at a 1953 Duke Ellington concert in London, England, with a chance meeting between John Meisel of Queen's department of political studies and Peter Harcourt, a young film enthusiast doing graduate work in English literature at Cambridge. The two became friends and, in the years that followed, kept in touch. Out of that correspondence came Harcourt's offhand comment that Queen's should provide instruction in film studies. As though his bluff had been called, Harcourt was given the job of developing the course, and in 1967, he began teaching film and English literature under the auspices of the English department at Queen's.

Initially taught simply as a tangent of literature, film studies moved out on its own in 1969. Harcourt, along with newly hired Professor Robin Wood, established a small department dedicated to communicating a thoughtful and comprehensive understanding of one of the 20th century's most powerful media. The department's graduates have since excelled in the highly competitive entertainment industry, proving the wisdom of the course that Harcourt and Wood set. Begun, like so many other disciplines at Queen's, in a University-owned house, the tiny effort has become an unqualified success.

Animation studio, film studies

Film studies graduates claimed Oscars in 1984 and 1987

Scripted unrest on the Lower Campus

Civil Government Service

For a time, during the first half of the 20th century, it seemed that the country's affairs had become a Queen's family business. Like parents passing on responsibilities to their children, successive generations of former professors working in Ottawa reached into the pool of talent that had passed through their Kingston classrooms and drew out young scholars eager to work in government. Indeed, beginning in 1908 with Adam Shortt — whose first assignment in Ottawa involved battling the traditional system of patronage and who later helped organize the Dominion Archives — the Queen's influence was integral to the beginnings of a modern, highly trained meritocracy in the civil service.

The scope of their impact was completely out of proportion to the tiny university from which they came. During Mackenzie King's term, O.D. Skelton, a former student of Adam Shortt's, earned such respect and influence as Under Secretary of State for External Affairs that he remained in the job even after the Conservatives, led by R.B. Bennett, came into power in 1930. His personal control over government operations and foreign affairs was enormous. Before any such position existed, he was referred to by many as the Deputy Prime Minister.

Perhaps his most lasting contribution was the introduction of open civil service competitions.

Skelton eventually conscripted W. Clifford Clark, a young professor at Queen's and a former student whom Skelton had taught during the years when Clark was earning full honours in five different subjects — Latin, French, English, history and political science. Clark, who became Deputy Minister of Finance and deserves much credit for the creation of the Bank of Canada, helped win the services of another young staff member, W.A. Mackintosh.

Although he served full-time in Ottawa only during World War II, Mackintosh held positions on a number of influential boards and commissions. In the Depression, he sat on the National Employment Commission, and during the war, he worked first for Clark and later for the redoubtable C.D. Howe. Unlike Shortt, Skelton and Clark, though, Mackintosh could not be enticed to abandon the academic world. When the war ended, he returned to Kingston, and in 1951, he became the first Queen's graduate ever chosen as Principal. Like so many other Queen's people, Mackintosh lent his talents to the government for a time but turned them once again to the University at Kingston.

Shortt, Skelton and Mackintosh

The construction of the Policy Studies Building at Queen's, officially opened in 1989, signalled the University's ongoing interest in government policy and the management of public affairs. In an effort to reunite areas of specialization that had grown out of a long-term focus on government activities, the University brought together several different centres of learning in one location: the School of Policy Studies, the School of Public Administration, the School of Industrial Relations, the Industrial Relations Centre, the School of Urban and Regional Planning, the John Deutsch Institute for the Study of Economic Policy, the Centre for International Relations and the Institute of Intergovernmental Relations.

The Aisles of History

In 1982, the heritage limestone building on the north side of The Medical Quadrangle behind Summerhill (formerly the New Medical Building) became the home for the administrative records and written traditions of Queen's as well as a staggering variety of archival material from across the country.

Maintained as an ''open-door repository,'' the Queen's University Archives, located in Kathleen Ryan Hall, allow researchers access to extensive collections. Included are the papers of such poets and writers as Archibald Lampman, E.J. Pratt, Stephen Leacock, Earle Birney, Dorothy Livesay and Al Purdy and the papers of national politicians and journalists, as well as the records of such companies as McLaughlin Carriage Company, the forerunner of General Motors of Canada. The Archives also contain photographs, sound recordings, architectural drawings and artifacts ranging from the medals of Sir Edward Peacock, a graduate who became financial advisor to the British Royal Family, to a hat that once belonged to poet Bliss Carman.

Such Queen's notables as Adam Shortt, who served as University librarian in the 1890s, and Principals Daniel Miner Gordon and John J. Deutsch have made significant contributions to the Archives. Lorne Pierce, who graduated from Queen's in 1912 and was editor of The Ryerson Press from 1920 to 1960, donated more than 1,000 items from his own collection of Canadian imprints and from the publications of The Ryerson Press. And the efforts of Leonard Brockington, Rector from 1947 to 1966, and benefactor Colonel R.S. McLaughlin brought Queen's the private papers of John Buchan, Lord Tweedsmuir and Governor General of Canada between 1935 and 1940.

The appointment of archivist Charles Beer in 1960 and of his successors in the years that followed ensured the proper organization of the vast collection, and the 1982 move into the fully equipped facilities at Kathleen Ryan Hall guaranteed that the ever-growing archival material would be guarded against the quiet ravages of time.

Kathleen Ryan Hall

19th-Century Treasure

In December 1841, the Royal Charter for Queen's College travelled from England to Kingston with the first official Principal, Reverend Thomas Liddell. The Charter consisted of three pages of sheepskin parchment with a braided pendant cord and included a wax seal the size of a small cake. Queen Victoria's official permission to commence the business of education arrived at Kingston in its travelling case, a long, narrow box with a large bulge built into it to accommodate the seal. The Charter promptly became the new university's most treasured artifact, stored away for posterity.

In 1989, archivists carefully unrolled the Charter from its case to restore it. They stretched the brittle document flat and painstakingly reconstructed the seal, which time had cracked and flaked.

More than three miles of documents line the Archives' shelves

A Very Public Woman

As a young woman during the years of World War I, Charlotte Whitton, Ottawa's future mayor, blazed through Queen's with the same fierce energy that she brought to everything she did. Arriving at the University with scholarships in six subjects, she graduated in 1917 with a master's degree and medals in history and English. While at Queen's, she won her University letters in field hockey, ice hockey and basketball; she served on the Levana Championship Debating Team in 1914-15, was associate editor of the *Queen's Journal* and was later the newspaper's first woman editor.

Whitton had style. Upon graduating, she became a crusader for children's rights and helped build the Canadian Council on Child Welfare. She earned a reputation as a leading expert on social welfare and was commissioned by Prime Minister R.B. Bennett in 1932 to study unemployment relief in the West. In 1947, Whitton drew charges of defamatory libel from the Alberta government after she accused the province of "bootlegging babies" to the United States — a subsequent investigation of adoption practices supported her criticisms.

In 1950, she stepped easily from social work into politics, when an *Ottawa Journal* editorial called her bluff following a speech in which she criticized the absence of women in public life. She promptly got herself elected senior member of the city's Board of Control, receiving more votes than any of the men running. When Mayor Grenville Goodwin died in office a few months later, Whitton became the first woman mayor in Canada. She then won reelection four times, in 1952, 1954, 1960 and 1962.

Whitton's diminutive size — she stood a shade over five feet — and her sharp, sometimes derisive, wit made her a ready target for every cartoonist and commentator in the country. Her notoriety tended to overshadow her effectiveness — her loud voice was legendary, and some believe she might have been named Ambassador to Ireland but for an incident in which she kicked a city controller in the shin and then followed up with a couple of punches. "There was no one there man enough to knock him down, so I tried to," she explained. Just the same, she ran a successful civic administration and earned a rare reputation for honesty and competence. She conducted one reelection campaign with an inimitable Whitton slogan, which simply promised "More of the Same."

Queen's remained important to Whitton long after she graduated. A onetime resident of Avonmore, she became a driving force behind the movement to establish a women's residence on campus. She served on the University's Board of Trustees from 1928 to 1940. And in 1941, she received an honorary degree from her alma mater.

(Queen's was graced by the presence and generosity of another member of Whitton's family, her sister Kathleen. In 1976, Kathleen Ryan marked the 50th anniversary of her graduation from Queen's with the endowment of a fund to provide for the preservation of buildings in The Medical Quadrangle behind Summerhill. In her honour, the building that houses Queen's University Archives is named Kathleen Ryan Hall.)

"None is a stranger path," Whitton once observed, "than that of a woman ranging in a world hitherto deemed a male preserve." Armed with intellect, education and a potent sense of humour, Whitton walked every path with confidence. She died in 1975 at the age of 78.

"Whatever women do, they must do twice as well as men to be thought half as good. Luckily, it's not difficult."

— Charlotte Whitton

The windows of the Agnes Craine Building reflect Kathleen Ryan Hall

Graduates leaving Queen's University travel in every direction, on every kind of road. They spread out across Canada; they move to new countries; in many cases, they return to homes overseas. They take up jobs that their professors could never have imagined, and their lives bring them a variety of experiences unknown among the orderly rites of campus and academe. In time, the memory of Queen's remains the single common thread tying them together. And since many cherish their membership in the University's broad community, the Alumni Association of Queen's University exists as a means of maintaining communication between the University and its supporters and graduates.

Formed in 1927 after an endowment campaign uncovered widespread support for the idea of such a group, the General Alumni Association of Queen's University began with a few straightforward commitments. On the cover of the first issue of its publication, *The Queen's Review* (now called the *Queen's Alumni Review*), the Alumni Association announced its pledge to "foster a spirit of loyalty, fraternity and help among the graduates and past students of Queen's University and to bring about united and concentrated action in promoting the welfare and advancing the interests, influence and usefulness of the University."

By 1990, the number of Queen's alumni had topped 78,000, and with more than 60 years of experience, the *Queen's Alumni Review* had become the means by which generations of graduates satisfied their curiosity, expressed their opinions or simply found an ongoing focus for their interest in Queen's.

Through the process of keeping up ties among alumni, the association also learned to sustain graduates' connections to their alma mater. Prompted by its original commitment to the serious business of promoting the interests of the University, the Alumni Association became a far-flung organization of more than 60 local chapters able to mobilize for fund raising. In addition, it established the channels of communication through which Queen's discusses its needs with graduates whose positions of influence have made them essential representatives of the University's interests in the halls of Canadian corporate and governmental power.

Alumnae

Long before the General Alumni Association, there was the Queen's University Alumnae Association. Formed at the turn of the century, the group faltered during its early years but gained new life and purpose in 1911 when women graduates decided to build an on-campus residence for female students. The alumnae pioneered the idea of Queen's people organizing in order to benefit the University. They established lines of communication among women graduates and not only raised money but also closely supervised the planning, material purchases, construction and eventual administration of Ban Righ Hall. Between 1916 and 1940, they published *The Alumnae News*, an annual jour-

nal devoted to the interests of women graduates of Queen's and to keeping abreast of such campus matters as the appointment of Hilda Laird as the new Dean of Women in 1925.

Although relieved of some of its responsibilities by the formation of the General Alumni Association, the Alumnae continued to shape women's affairs at Queen's through the considerable influence of such bodies as the Ban Righ Foundation and the Marty-Royce and Lynett Scholarship Committees. In the spring of 1990, the Alumnae Association was absorbed by the Alumni Association and became known as the Committee on Women's Affairs, retaining both its focus and its responsibilities.

Alumni Weekend welcome, a recent sign of autumn

Orientation

It is like a party hosted by a good-humoured maniac who opens the front door for each guest and screams, ''Welcome. Come in.'' Some people are thrilled by the greeting, and some are seriously offended. Every September, upper-year students receive frosh at Queen's with a boisterousness that cannot be ignored, an uninhibited goodwill intended to melt away shyness and reserve. Orientation is a week of frivolity and of tedious registration paperwork, but it is also a week in which a constantly changing campus population receives and renews its powerful sense of community.

Breaking the tedium of registration

Exploring the streets of Kingston during orientation week

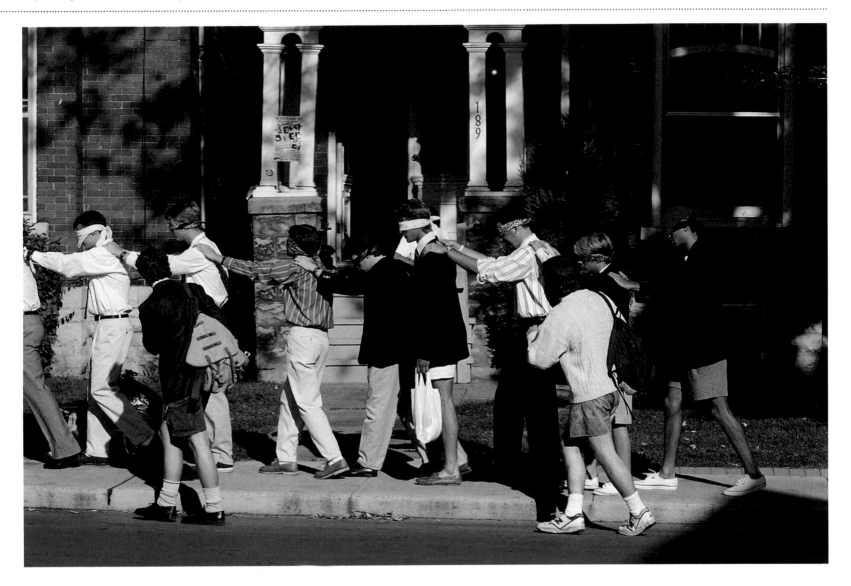

Sartorial chaos ended on the gridiron with the adoption in 1884 of the official tricolour

''When our number was small, it was perhaps judicious not to wear any distinguishing mark, as it would have shown that paucity too plainly. Now, however, that the undergraduates have so increased that the old buildings are no longer able to hold them, why should we not have some mark by which we should know each other, and the citizens, generally, know us?''
— *Queen's College Journal*, February 21, 1880

Line of scrimmage, Richardson Stadium

Red, blue and yellow have served as the familiar tricolours of the Queen's community for more than a century. They have adorned every imaginable surface — from faces to flagpoles, cars, scarves and tam-o'-shanters. They have become, in short, synonymous with Queen's. But before the 1880s, there was no consensus whatsoever about what colours should signify the school; even the athletic teams presented a hodgepodge. An editorial in the *Queen's College Journal*, February 21, 1880, offered this advice, ''We might suggest to the officers of the Snow Shoe and the Football Clubs, in case they determine to select colours, to meet and decide on the same that the colours may not represent the clubs so much as the College; the form of the wearing will be sufficient to distinguish the clubs.''

In 1884, a committee was at last convened to bring order to the sartorial chaos that reigned whenever Queen's teams took to the field. The familiar tricolours were chosen from the Queen's crest, which in turn had been patterned on the coat of arms of the University of Edinburgh. The decision came just in time. The football team of 1883 had early on determined to wear dark red stockings, white knickerbockers and dark blue jerseys but had reduced the whole issue to utter confusion later in the season by switching to black stockings and then to blue jerseys, dark trousers and red polo caps.

The colours were set down in the words of the original Queen's yell: ''*Dearg, gor'mus, buidthe! / Oil-thigh na Banrighinn gu brath! / Cha Gheill! Cha Gheill! Cha Gheill!*''—''Red! Blue! Yellow! / Queen's forever! / No surrender! No surrender! No surrender!''

Queen's first physical-training instructor — retired Colonel Angus Cameron — preferred exercises "of a military nature, with dumbbells and clubs, as in the army." As far as Cameron was concerned, the alternative — "throwing a heavy hammer or caber" — seemed of little use at all.

Victorian attitudes toward health and physical fitness had changed by the late 19th century, but in 1857, when Colonel Cameron wrote to the Board of Trustees suggesting that physical activity was good for students, he also proposed that it be "retired from jeering spectators." Jumping about and perspiring in public were apparently not altogether seemly.

What he won for students amounted to no more than some "vaulting crossbars, ladder ropes and a few other items," but to Colonel Cameron, who made himself available three or four hours per week in a gymnastics room in Summerhill, goes the credit for initiating athletics at Queen's.

"One great defect was the absence of all gymnastic or calisthenic exercises. Frequently, the writer left the college work, after hours of closest application, with a severe pain in his head and a sense of great weariness and exhaustion only to walk slowly and quietly home, to resume his wearing mental toil, conscious that a game of ball or cricket would have been of incalculable advantage, both to body and mind, yet prevented by fear that such a liberty would have been considered unbecoming his dignity as a student for the ministry or by the fact that such was the general view taken of public opinion by his fellow students and that they never attempted to transgress in this matter."
— Minute Book, the Dialectic Society of Queen's College, 1843-55

Athletics in 1857 were restricted to dumbbells and crossbars

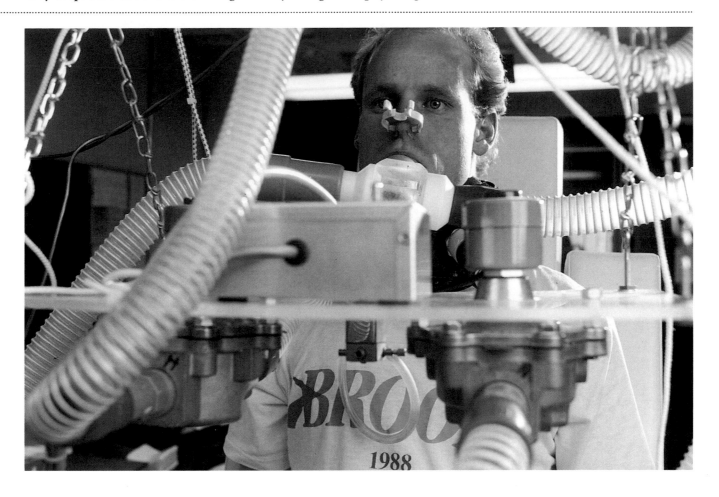

"Do we not want hardy and energetic
men for Ministers, Doctors and
Lawyers?"

— *Queen's College Journal*, 1874

In 1957, with almost a century of frustrated attempts behind it, Queen's was finally able to open its doors to law students. Toronto's Osgoode Hall Law School, which had until then held a monopoly on the teaching of law in Ontario, had at last relinquished its power.

As early as the 1860s, students attending law courses offered by Queen's had become understandably discouraged. At that time, the Law Society of Upper Canada required that all lawyers receive three years of training at the society's own school, Osgoode Hall, to be followed by a year of articles. Training received elsewhere did not affect the length of time a student was expected to "do terms" in Toronto. It is not surprising that the Queen's operation folded after three years of desultory enrolment, amidst confusion about the arrangement of the faculty and a good deal of discontent concerning payments to the lecturers, most of whom were practising local lawyers. An attempted revival in the 1880s came to a similar end.

Following World War II, however, returning veterans produced a marked increase in the number of aspiring lawyers. Unable to meet the demand and under pressure from institutions like the University of Toronto, the Law Society of Upper Canada eventually agreed to share the field of legal education. Although the changeover involved years of bitter controversy, Queen's Principal W.A. Mackintosh maintained a good relationship with the Law Society "Benchers." His quiet diplomacy contrasted with the harsh criticism levelled by others, and once they had decided upon a programme of sanctioned studies, Queen's was among the first to establish an independent Faculty of Law.

In a reenactment of the University's humble beginnings, the law school began in temporary quarters in a house owned by Queen's and scheduled for demolition. In September 1957, the faculty's original three professors — Stuart Ryan, Daniel A. Soberman and James Alexander Corry — welcomed the first 25 students. Later that year, William R. Lederman was persuaded to take on the job of Dean. The Faculty of Law was thus under way, or as Vice-Principal Corry commented, "Assuming that interludes of 70 years are unimportant in the life of a university, it would be more correct to say that the Trustees agreed to the resuming of instruction in the Queen's Faculty of Law."

Sir John A. Macdonald: Legal Aid

Sir John A. Macdonald Hall, which houses the Faculty of Law, opened in the fall of 1960. Almost 100 years after ambitious founders first considered the idea, the study of law at Queen's finally found its own home. Naming the building after Canada's first Prime Minister also served to acknowledge the contributions that Macdonald had made to the Scottish Presbyterian College in his home city of Kingston. Never associated with Queen's in any official capacity, Macdonald nevertheless provided active support throughout his life. Early on, his legal opinion was often sought, and later in his career, he proved generous in the use of his powers to assist

Queen's. Macdonald was present in 1839 at the meeting called to discuss the proposed college and, in fact, put forward one of the resolutions adopted.

Macdonald went on to assist with the founding of the Queen's medical school and continued to give assistance to an institution that sometimes faltered but never failed. His moral support was reinforced with financial contributions, and Queen's library often benefited from his kindness. The law building was a fitting commemoration not only because of Macdonald's profession but also because a century before, Macdonald's partner, Alexander Campbell, had served as the Dean of Queen's first law school.

William R. Lederman, Queen's first Dean of Law

John James Deutsch (1968-74): The Great Communicator

Born in 1911, John Deutsch, the eldest of 17 children, began life on the Saskatchewan prairies. His Bavarian father and Hungarian mother were homesteaders on a piece of land north of Regina, 50 miles from the railroad and the nearest town.

By the time Deutsch entered Queen's in 1933, the 21-year-old was already an experienced high school teacher with enough extramural university credits to step into a Bachelor of Commerce programme. While supporting himself teaching at Kingston's Regiopolis College, he completed his degree in just two years. After doing graduate work in 1936, he began a career in the federal civil service. In the words of Peter C. Newman in *The Canadian Establishment*, Deutsch became "probably the most remarkable and certainly the most practical of the great Ottawa mandarins."

Deutsch believed firmly in the link between academic research and economic policy, and his own career demonstrated the fruitful blend of scholarship and worldly endeavour. He became a professor of economics at Queen's and, later, a professor of economics and head of the department of economics and political science at the University of British Columbia. He also served on the boards of several companies, including the Aluminum Co. of Canada Ltd. (Alcan) and the Canadian Imperial Bank of Commerce. He was Vice-Principal of Queen's from 1959 to 1963, and throughout his career, he also served on some of the most powerful commissions in the federal government, including the Economic Council of Canada, which he chaired through its first four years, beginning in 1963. He became Principal of Queen's in 1968, crowning a long and happy association with his alma mater.

A man with wisdom and an international perspective, Deutsch suited the role of a university principal. His great talent as an administrator and his wide experience proved essential to Queen's after so many years of unbridled progress. Calling a halt to expansion, he undertook the tricky business of consolidating the extensive gains the University had made since World War II. Deutsch pointed out that Queen's would trade away too much of value by attempting to be all things to all people. In an age of mega-universities, he strove to keep Queen's in touch with its tradition as a smaller institution intent on safeguarding high standards of instruction. In view of the years of growth, Deutsch realized that that also meant redefining the University's relations with the City of Kingston, with other universities and with government.

Deutsch's concern for the ways in which people communicate extended far beyond the simple processes of administration. An appreciation of his personal charm was recorded on the plaque installed in the foyer of the John Deutsch University Centre, dedicated on October 22, 1977: "Educator, public servant, advisor to industry, John J. Deutsch, Principal and Vice-Chancellor 1968-74, guided Queen's wisely through a period of growth and change. The centre, incorporating the Students' Memorial Union, is a tribute to his warm humanity, his rapport with students and his dedication to the purposes of the centre."

Principal John J. Deutsch

A spring break, outside the John Deutsch University Centre

"The possibility of faith, after all, is
the essence of the human condition."
— John James Deutsch

In 1961, the march of progress at Queen's ran headlong into campus tradition. Since World War II, the Board of Trustees, which had wrestled with the problem of locating new buildings on the increasingly crowded University grounds, had avoided excavating the green space south of Kingston Hall. In 1945, Principal Robert C. Wallace had determined that the area should be preserved "both for aesthetic reasons and because of the need of the open space for playing grounds." The attempted reversal of that decision 16 years later set off a fierce debate.

The decision by Principal W.A. Mackintosh and the Trustees to locate a new physics building on the Lower Campus brought sharp, immediate criticism. Professor Arthur Lower of the department of history led the fight, but the *Queen's Journal* quickly joined in with editorial commentary upon "The Rape of Lower Campus." Petitions sponsored by the Levana Society were circulated, and demonstrators held a mock funeral at which they sang *Oil Thigh* as a dirge. Alumni entered the fray on both sides, and the Faculty Association contributed its own strong criticism of the site, thereby bringing the whole Lower Campus plan to a confused halt.

An unlikely saviour, the University's realtor, Graham Thomson, eventually resolved the issue by assembling purchase options for property along Queen's Crescent, in the neighbourhood of the Lower Campus but not on it. Presented with an alternative space large enough to hold the new physics building, later known as Stirling Hall after former Chancellor J.B. Stirling, the Board of Trustees eagerly reversed its decision. Few controversies end with such unanimous accord.

"Chuck Edwards — where are you today?"

— "A Eulogy for Student Movement," *Queen's Journal*, 1978

"Radicals" on Campus

Radicalism. In the words of the 1971-72 Alma Mater Society vice-president, Victor Bradley, "Queen's was the last to get it and the first to lose it." During the tumultuous 1960s and early 1970s, the Edwards Case of 1970 constituted the only serious clash between Queen's students and their administration.

Charles Edwards, a member of the Free Socialist Movement, claimed that his doctoral supervisor, Professor Henry Becker, had forced him to choose between his academic work in the department of chemical engineering and his political activities. The serious accusation prompted a full-blown enquiry, including public hearings conducted by Bernard L. Adell, Associate Dean of Law. Twenty-eight sessions lasting more than 90 hours were required to hear the testimony of 17 witnesses.

The Adell report described Becker as "utterly innocent" of the charges Edwards had brought, but when the Senate met on March 11 to consider its response, members of the Free Socialist Movement crashed the closed meeting and forced it to be rescheduled as a public forum. On April 3, that public meeting took place in Wallace Hall in the Students' Memorial Union and was broadcast on the campus radio station. Edwards, although "strongly censured," was "permitted the opportunity of formulating and having accepted by the ordinary academic processes an alternate plan of academic study within Queen's University."

Playing-field aesthetics, the Lower Campus

Some things never change. Like the Grant Hall tower, some rooms, buildings and vistas at Queen's have survived the evolution of the campus, protected by the unshakable affection of students, faculty and alumni. But in most cases, progress at a university like Queen's is bittersweet. Each new building fills an open space or displaces old student houses or even the spacious faculty homes of another era. With each permutation, traditions shift and memories fade. Fortunately, even nostalgia possesses vigour, and each time the face of the campus changes, a new generation of students takes it to its heart.

Campus in the making; Kingston Hall and Grant Hall, circa 1918

The view down University Avenue: Douglas Library, Ontario Hall and Grant Hall

R.L. Watts (1974-84): Leader From Within

Ronald Lampman Watts earned a reputation as a Principal in touch with student and campus concerns, and it is easy to see how. When he became Principal, he was already steeped in the University's academic, administrative and student traditions. A Rhodes Scholar who was appointed to the staff in 1955 as a lecturer in political philosophy, he also became the first don and warden of McNeill House, the new men's residence. The older generation that influenced his progress — both intellectually and within the Queen's community — included former Principals W.A. Mackintosh, J.A. Corry and John J. Deutsch.

Watts became a full professor in political studies in 1965 and served as Dean of Arts and Science from 1969 to 1974. In 1974, at the age of 45, he became the youngest Queen's Principal since Reverend George Monro Grant accepted the job almost a century earlier. As a Principal, Watts was a product of Queen's own system, prepared by nearly 20 years in the community that he was eventually to lead.

Heading for class

Referring to the honour and respect accorded the leader of a great university, Ronald Watts describes his own tenure as Principal of Queen's with a quote from Sir Winston Churchill: "The nation had the lion's heart. I had the luck to give the roar." He views his period of being so closely identified with the prestige of the University as a mark of his own good fortune. And he downplays the position's power, referring to the Principal as simply the head professor, someone who, as Watts did, remains a teacher.

Compared with the wartime career of Wallace or with the Mackintosh and Corry years of explosive growth at Queen's, Watts' time as Principal would have appeared, to an impartial observer, a relatively quiet period, a decade occasionally punctuated by student complaints about inadequate funding and by less frequent but more serious confrontations over the ethical implications of some of Queen's financial investments. Principal Watts served on powerful government committees — the Bovey Commission and the Task Force on Canadian Unity — a reflection both of the University's eminence and of the personal respect he commanded, but progress at Queen's was not as sensational.

The quiet, however, was deceptive. During those years, something less dramatic than international hostilities was going on; something less substantial but more enduring than new buildings was taking shape. The University's traditional commitments and very self-perception were being reaffirmed and strengthened. To Watts fell Principal John J. Deutsch's task of reining in the tumbling momentum of previous years and reshaping patterns of growth that had begun to threaten Queen's with the kind of gigantism that ruins many universities. Difficult decisions were made. Enrolment was limited even while the short supply of government funds remained tagged to student numbers. The pressure to grow could not be allowed to undermine the University's high standards, and so limits were established in spite of the demands of all those who felt that their particular departments should continue to grow. Notwithstanding the successful $13.5 million Queen's Quest fund-raising drive and the launch of the Queen's Appeal, the University struggled financially. The belt was drawn so tightly that amidst the predictable jokes about Watts and kilowatts, stickers appeared beside light switches entreating people to "turn off for Queen's."

If anything, slowing the growth of a large institution is more demanding than the exhausting task of expansion. The economic difficulties must be handled with the deftest diplomacy, and preserving Queen's style and intimate scale was a task no less harrowing in its way than piloting a ship by night through treacherous shoals. Yet Watts (the Principal known for his love of sailing) steered the University with the kind of graceful ease that gave the impression of sailing upon the calmest seas. Under Watts, Queen's at long last emerged from the postwar boom, and it is due largely to the decisions made during his tenure that the University's commitments to quality and a national outlook remained intact. That is the message of the quiet "roar" that Ronald Watts gave.

David C. Smith (1984-   ): Toward Another 150 Years

During the first 150 years of its history, Queen's has seen the Principal evolve from a Presbyterian clergyman — the Primarius Professor of Theology who knew most or all of the school's students by name and who devoted vast amounts of time to campaigning for funds — to an extraordinarily competent secular administrator. The Principal today has an annual budget of approximately $300 million and supervises the affairs of nearly 13,000 students each year and more than 3,000 staff and faculty, as well as fund raising.

One other essential characteristic of the Principal has remained constant through the years. For each Principal, Queen's has selected a renowned scholar, a true and fitting leader of the academic community. David C. Smith's appointment in 1984 reaffirmed that tradition. After undergraduate study at McMaster University, Smith earned a master's at Oxford and a Ph.D. in economics at Harvard and was elected a Fellow of the Royal Society of Canada. Prior to his arrival at Queen's department of economics in 1960, he held a faculty position at the University of California, Berkeley. As department head between 1968 and 1981, Smith oversaw Queen's growing international reputation for the study of economics.

Principal David C. Smith, the Collins Room, Richardson Hall

The Friendless and the Orphaned

"In the hope of finding some guidance, I read the Queen's installation addresses over the past century, many of them delivered in this hall. My predecessors had their qualms too.

"A thread of apprehension about the financial problems to be faced weaves through their speeches with much contemporary relevance, and the need to cultivate a careful style of negativism is recognized. Thus it was said approvingly of one Principal that he had learned to say no — encouragingly. The strains of a principalship on close personal relationships are recognized, and two refer to the complaint of a university president's wife that 'the only people who should be university presidents are the friendless, the orphaned and bachelors.'

"Some reassurance is found in the observation that Queen's has a great capacity to survive its Principals. Thus W.A. Mackintosh at his installation observed:

" 'What anxieties I have are lessened because I am sensible of the fact that Queen's University at Kingston is not to be made or destroyed by any Principal. She is a living thing in which the Principal is a prominent, visible, too frequently audible, but not absolutely vital organ.'

"But one finds in these speeches, too, the sense of excitement which I share this evening about being part of the Queen's mission. And I have the advantage of being able to follow on the courses charted so well by my distinguished predecessors, four of whom I have known and worked under: Principals Mackintosh, Corry, Deutsch and Watts."
— from an address given October 26, 1984, by David C. Smith on the occasion of his installation as Principal and Vice-Chancellor of Queen's University

Douglas Library, built 1924

On April 27-28, 1881, Founders' Avenue was laid out from the gate at the head of George Street to the main entrance of the Old Arts Building, now Theological Hall. A sapling was ostensibly planted in the name of each of the founding patrons by a relative or representative. Although over the years, some of the trees succumbed to age and to heavy winds off the lake, others of the living commemorations to Queen's founders still survive, grown to maturity, their greenery and grand stature dominating the eastern half of the Lower Campus.

Index

Honours science class of 1888

Credits

Page 5 Alan Carruthers; p.6 Ernie Sparks; p. 7 Cavouk; p.9 Queen's Picture Collection (QPC), Queen's Archives (QA); p. 10 J.A. Kraulis; p. 12 J.A. Kraulis; p. 13 Alan Carruthers; p. 15 QPC, QA; p. 16 J.A. Kraulis; p. 18 QPC, QA; p. 19 J.A. Kraulis; p. 20 J.A. Kraulis; p. 22 QPC, QA; p. 23 Jack Chiang; p. 24 J.A. Kraulis; p. 25 QPC, QA; p. 27 Alumni Picture Collection (APC), QA; p. 28 J.A. Kraulis; p. 29 Alan Carruthers; p. 30 J.A. Kraulis; p. 31 QPC, QA; p. 33 J.A. Kraulis; p. 34 Kathleen Ryan Collection, QPC, QA; p. 35 APC, QA; p. 36 J.A. Kraulis; p. 37 Sheldon Davis, QPC, QA; p. 38 (left to right) J.W. Powell, QPC, QA; QPC, QA; QPC, QA; QPC,QA; p. 41 QPC, QA; p. 42 Alan Carruthers; p. 43 QPC, QA; p. 44 Alan Carruthers; p. 45 Hal Steacy Collection, QA; p. 46 J.A. Kraulis; p. 47 Alan Carruthers; p. 48 J.A. Kraulis; p. 49 Alan Carruthers; p. 50 Alan Carruthers; p. 51 Michael Lea, courtesy Kingston *Whig-Standard*; p. 53 J.A. Kraulis; p. 54 Alan Carruthers; p. 55 QPC, QA; p. 56 APC, QA; p. 57 APC, QA; p. 58 APC, QA; p. 59 Alan Carruthers; p. 60 QPC, QA; p. 61 Alan Carruthers; p. 63 (top) Alan Carruthers, (bottom) Mildred Clow Collection, QPC, QA; p. 64 Alan Carruthers; p.65 Alan Carruthers; p. 67 Alan Carruthers; p. 69 APC, QA; p. 70 Alan Carruthers; p. 71 QPC, QA; p. 72 Alan Carruthers; p. 73 Alan Carruthers; p. 74 QPC, QA; p. 75 Alan Carruthers; p. 76 Alan Carruthers; p. 77 QPC, QA; p. 78 Alan Carruthers; p. 79 Alan Carruthers; p. 80 J.A. Kraulis; p. 81 National Archives of Canada (C14128); p. 82 Alan Carruthers; p. 83 QPC, QA; p. 85 W. Sellar Collection, QPC, QA; p. 86 courtesy Elspeth Baugh; p. 87 Alan Carruthers; p. 88 Alan Carruthers; p. 89 Alan Carruthers; p. 90 APC, QA; p. 91 APC, QA; p. 92 J.A. Kraulis; p. 93 QPC, QA; p. 95 APC, QA; p. 96 A.E. O'Kane Collection, QPC, QA; p. 97 J.A. Kraulis; p. 98 J.A. Kraulis; p. 99 Alan Carruthers; p. 100 courtesy Agnes McCausland Benedickson; p. 101 APC, QA; p. 102 Alan Carruthers; p. 103 QPC, QA; p. 104 QPC, QA; p. 105 Alan Carruthers; p. 106 Alan Carruthers; p. 107 J.A. Kraulis; p. 108 Alan Carruthers; p. 109 J.A. Kraulis; p. 110 Alan Carruthers; p. 111 Alan Carruthers; p. 112 J.A. Kraulis; p. 113 Alan Carruthers; p. 114 Alan Carruthers; p. 115 Alan Carruthers; p. 117 J.A Kraulis; p. 118 QPC, QA; p. 119 J.A. Kraulis; p. 120 QPC, QA; p. 121 APC, QA; p. 122 Alan Carruthers; p. 123 J.A. Kraulis; p. 124 Alan Carruthers; p. 125 J.A. Kraulis; p. 127 Ernie Sparks; p. 128 Alan Carruthers; p. 129 Alan Carruthers; p. 130 Alan Carruthers; p. 132 J.A. Kraulis; p. 133 Alan Carruthers; p. 134 QPC, QA; p. 135 Alan Carruthers; p. 136 Alan Carruthers; p. 137 George Lilley Collection, QA; p. 138 J.A. Kraulis; p. 139 Alan Carruthers; p. 140 Alan Carruthers; p. 141 Alan Carruthers; p. 142 Alan Carruthers; p. 143 Alan Carruthers; p. 144 Alan Carruthers; p. 146 Alan Carruthers; p. 147 Alan Carruthers; p. 148 (left to right) QPC, QA; Canadian Government Motion Picture Bureau, QPC, QA; QPC, QA; p. 149 J.A. Kraulis; p. 150 J.A. Kraulis; p. 151 Alan Carruthers; p. 153 J.A. Kraulis; p. 154 Alan Carruthers; p. 155 Alan Carruthers; p. 156 Alan Carruthers; p. 157 Alan Carruthers; p. 158 Alan Carruthers; p. 159 Alan Carruthers; p. 160 Alan Carruthers; p. 161 Alan Carruthers; p. 162 J.A. Kraulis; p. 163 Alan Carruthers; p. 164 Doug MacDonald Collection, QPC, QA; p. 165 Alan Carruthers; p. 166 George Lilley Collection, QA; p. 167 Alan Carruthers; p. 168 QPC, QA; p. 169 J.A. Kraulis; p. 170 J.A. Kraulis; p. 172 Alan Carruthers; p. 173 J.A. Kraulis; p. 174 Alan Carruthers; p. 177 APC, QA; p. 179 Michael Lea, courtesy Kingston *Whig-Standard*.

Polishing up for exams, Jock Harty Arena